C000118248

To Helen

With my love and very best wishes

Keith

December 2008

Ernest Hayes

Brass in the Golden Age

Keith Booth

With a foreword by Mark Ramprakash

First published in Great Britain by
Association of Cricket Statisticians and Historians
Cardiff CF11 9XR
© ACS, 2008

British Library Cataloguing-in-Publication Data.
A catalogue record for this book is available from the British
Library.

ISBN: 978 1 905138 68 5
Typeset by Limlow Books

Contents

Foreword

By Mark Ramprakash

Batting at No.3 is always a challenge. You can find yourself facing the second ball of the match, or at the other end of the scale, going in to push the score along, having waited with the pads on for several hours while the openers notch up 300 or so.

There is, of course, now no one in the Surrey dressing room, or even the committee room, who saw Ernie Hayes play cricket and very few to whom the name means anything at all, but the record books don't lie and 27,000 plus first-class runs and 48 centuries say that Hayes must have had the versatility required to bat in that No 3 spot which he occupied for most of his career, much of it in the shadow of openers Jack Hobbs and Tom Hayward.

As I said on a number of occasions to the media this year, any century is special and it may well be that they were even more special in Hayes' time. There was more first-class cricket then, so there were more opportunities, but it has also to be remembered that pitches were uncovered and runs perhaps harder to acquire than they are on the batsman-friendly surfaces of today.

Modern cricketers often complain about playing too much cricket and too much travelling, with not enough time for recovery and practice in between. But we do have sponsored cars, a network of motorways, decent hotels and are reasonably well paid. We can only admire at a distance the old professionals, like Ernie Hayes, who a hundred years ago played six days a week, travelled everywhere by public transport, stayed in often quite basic accommodation, endured long sea voyages to play abroad and were often dependent on a successful benefit to ensure a decent standard of living when they had retired from the game.

It is all too easy to disregard our heritage and ancestry and to forget those who have gone before, but Keith's book throws light on another age, reminds us of where we've come from and helps us realise how fortunate we are to be where we are today.

Preface

Shortly after the publication of my biography of George Lohmann, I found myself being asked by a number of people what my next project was to be. When I replied that it would possibly be Ernest Hayes, the reaction, even from Surrey members and supporters with an interest in and knowledge of the history of the club, was, 'Who?' Yet Hayes played five hundred first-class matches for Surrey, a figure not approached by any current player and bettered by only five others. He scored 45 centuries for his county, and is now tenth in the all-time list, having this year moved down a place to accommodate the Ramprakash phenomenon.

History recalls him as being overshadowed by Hobbs and Hayward, but that is by no means how contemporary commentators saw him. His contribution, usually at No.3 in the Surrey order, was a significant one and he still features in a number of partnership and other Surrey records.

It is unlikely that the thought of a Hayes biography would have entered my head, had it not been for the depositing in the club archives of four scrapbooks by his family in the early nineties. They cover the whole of his playing career and provide a unique source of material for a chronicle of one who, in the words of the hymnologist, would have otherwise remained 'unknown and unrewarded'. Professional cricket has not until recently been the best rewarded of sports and there is nothing that can be done to change that history, but perhaps due to that chance discovery, Hayes may become slightly less unknown.

The scrapbooks, annotated with his own reminiscences, contain correspondence with a number of his distinguished contemporaries, and cover the whole of his first-class career and the bits before and afterwards. Although they are well maintained, the majority of the press items do not indicate the source and are not dated, except by season. Most, however, seem to be from *The Sportsman, Sporting Times, Cricket Star, Wisden, Cricket* magazine or local newspapers and the date can in a number of cases, be inferred from the context or the content of adjacent items. They give a fascinating insight into the life and times of a modest and unassuming man and one perhaps unappreciated and under-rated as a professional cricketer and contributor to society.

Ernest Hayes has had brief walk-on parts in three of my earlier books – as designer of the Ernie Hayes scorebook, as a visitor to George Lohmann and as a mourner at C.W.Alcock's funeral. The time has come for him to occupy centre-stage for a change, as well as adding a batsman to join a wicket-keeper, administrator and bowler in the author's canon of Surrey biography.

Keith Booth
Sutton, Surrey
October, 2008

Chapter One
Childhood and Early Cricket

'... the great Honor Oak players of the past, like Ernie Hayes ...
possibly the most famous of them all.'
Micky Stewart, in his Foreword to the *Honor Oak C.C. Centenary*
booklet, 1965

Ernest George Hayes was born on 6 November 1876, the youngest
of the five sons of Christopher, a master draper, later a hosier and
haberdasher, and Jane Hayes in Peckham, in the cricketing county
of Surrey, which, after several local government boundary
changes, now forms part of the London Borough of Southwark. He
died, aged 77, only a few miles away in West Norwood, so in the
words of Surrey spin doctors and PR people when they wish to
emphasize the merits of local managers and players against those
of upstart Australians and 'Kolpaks', he was 'Surrey through and
through'. There was, however, a lot of living in between.

His maternal grandfather was a cheesemonger; his paternal
grandfather a floor cloth manufacturer, the precursor of a
broader-ranging drapery and hosiery business, providing a family
background which was respectable lower middle-class. The family
had a penchant, well ahead of the Education Act of 1870, for
improvement and upward mobility, as demonstrated by Ernest's
father being sent to boarding school at St Nicholas' College at
Hurstpierpoint in Sussex.

In 1876, Queen Victoria was just over half way through her reign,
the Empire was approaching its zenith and, apart from a little
skirmish in the Crimea, Britain had been at peace since the
Napoleonic Wars and 'led the world'. The Boer War at the turn of
the century and two devastating World Wars before the half-way
point of the next one were to change all that and when Ernest
Hayes departed this life, just six months after the coronation of
the young Queen Elizabeth, Britain was a very different country. A
period of post-war recession and depression heralded the

dismantling of an Empire on which at his birth it was said the sun would never set.

The family home was 795 Old Kent Road, an epicentre of East End London, with the 1871 Census recording it as the residence of Christopher and Jane with Ernest's four elder brothers, Christopher, William, Charles and Arthur, aged at the time four, three, two and six months. There was a six-year age gap between the rest of the family and Ernest. The 1881 Census shows little change, except that Ernest is there now aged four, and the eldest brother Christopher Daniel, named after his father and, incidentally his grandfather, is visiting his uncle Robert Newham, one of his mother's eight siblings, in Chigwell. The presence of a domestic servant (not the same one) in both censuses suggests an existence two or three levels above the breadline. In his famous poverty survey of 1889, Charles Booth characterises this particular part of the Old Kent Road as 'middle class' and 'well to do'. Ernest's childhood home is no longer there, having been superseded by a 'Land of Leather' megastore.

Ernest was educated at East Dulwich College (or Grammar School, as the contemporary Post Office directory has it), a small commercial establishment on East Dulwich Grove at Carlton House, Southville Park Villas, with Mrs George Williams as its principal. It was an institution which seems to have provided him with the ability to write legibly in correct and understandable English, with almost infallible spelling and punctuation. He recalls

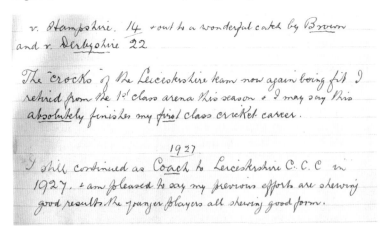

The scrapbooks were always carefully written, even after his cricket had ended.

playing cricket there and doing well, albeit against mediocre bowling.

By 1891, the family had moved to 121 Upland Road, also East Dulwich, a respectable two-up and two-down suburban residence. Ernest, now 14, was employed as a 'merchant's clerk', his father is described as a 'hosier and haberdasher', the eldest brother as a 'lace warehouseman' and the second brother, William, as a haberdasher. So there is a similarity and a continuity of occupation in the family. Strangely, after leaving school in his thirteenth year[1] in 1889, Ernest played no cricket for three years.

The Hayes family lived here in Upland Road, East Dulwich in the 1890s.

Later, the family moved to 42 Hollydale Road in Peckham, just south of Queen's Road. Again the house has been demolished, like his birthplace on the Old Kent Road, subjected to Southwark Borough Council's policies of 'inner city regeneration'. On the site stands St Thomas the Apostle Catholic College, *alma mater* of current Ipswich Town footballer, Danny Haynes.

Hayes' early cricket, other than that at school, was with the Honor Oak Club, established as The Star Cricket Club in 1866 and changing its name in 1887. It is still extant, though now merged with Old Alleynians to form Edward Alleyn and Honor Oak Cricket Club and playing in the fourth tier of the Surrey Championship. For much of Hayes' long association with Honor Oak, it was one of the leading clubs in South London.

---

1   The school-leaving age under the 1870 Act was 13, with some exemptions in agricultural areas.

Honor Oak: 1892 to 1894

He joined the Honor Oak Club in 1892 at the age of 15 and remained a member until his death more than 60 years later. In those early days the Club played at Colyton Road, East Dulwich, having relocated there from Peckham Rye in 1884. It was not until 1932 that it moved to its present location at Dulwich Common on London's South Circular Road. His elder brother Christopher Daniel played with Honor Oak's second eleven.

It is at this point that the scrapbooks begin. In beautifully legible script, Hayes records: 'Having first started playing cricket regularly in 1892 age 15½ years, following is outline of performances for that season and following ones up to 1895 (full account being written in previous books).'

Those 'previous books' have not survived.

He had earlier been scorer, but now began scoring runs with his bat rather than his pencil and in that first season, showed early promise with 577 runs – mainly for the second eleven – at an average of 44.38, precipitating a reference as 'a young cricketer who bids fair to become a Lohmann or a Streatfeild'. It was only the previous year that F.H.Huish had joined the Club. He was later to keep wicket for Kent, playing almost 500 first-class matches.

The following season, the young Hayes held a regular first eleven place and was second in the averages to Honor Oak stalwart and future captain, G.S.Harrison. In 1894, adding leg-spin bowling to his now well-established right-hand batting skills, he topped the batting and bowling averages in a season epitomised by an all-round performance on August Bank Holiday Monday when he made 65 and took six wickets against Hornsey Rise. His scrapbook records:

> I now come to what is no doubt the most successful, up to the present, cricket season I have had. Playing throughout all the matches for the first eleven at the finish of the season I was top in the batting by thirteen points and also top in the bowling averages. This latter was an unlooked-for surprise and my success no doubt came about through having been bowled more than previous years and thus gaining experience and confidence.

He had already attracted Surrey's attention and played for the Young Professionals against the Young Amateurs, scoring 33.

Honor Oak and Surrey: 1895

1895 was even better. Hayes accumulated 1,002 runs at an average of 58.94, both club records at the time. Hornsey Rise again suffered at his hands. His seven for 25 was principally responsible for their dismissal for 70. He then opened the batting, as he did regularly that season, with T.R.Dickason, and scored 185, also a record for an individual innings. The opening partnership of 251 established yet another record, eclipsing the same pair's 172 against Clapton. By the end of the season, Surrey were beginning to take a more serious interest and sent along W.T.Graburn, the cricket instructor, to see him play and, as a result, selected Hayes for five of the county's second-eleven matches in August. In five innings he scored 331 runs and was asked to sign as a professional, being engaged as a 'ground bowler'.

Hayes, aged 19, in a fast-fading Honor Oak first eleven of 1895.
Back row (l to r): A.Percy (scorer), E.G.Hayes, W.E.Tapp, E.Chapman,
T.R.Dickason, J.Gadd (umpire).
Middle row: H.H.Burton, A.Jones (wk), G.S.Harrison (capt), F.A.Wilkie,
H.L.Holford.
On the ground: J.Johnson, F.F.Harrison.

A local newspaper applauded the policy of using county second-eleven fixtures to provide emerging young players with valuable experience, and singled out Hayes as an example of one whose selection on this basis would benefit both himself and the club:

13

Latterly the policy of the executive seems to have rightly been to dispense as much as possible with the services of those who are standing out of the first team for whatever reason, so that the second eleven may be fully representative of the rising young cricketers of the county. In the latest addition to the second team, E.G.Hayes, who comes from Honor Oak C.C., Surrey seems to have a young batsman of more than ordinary promise. . . . Not yet twenty-one, with more experience he should develop into a very useful cricketer.

On his first appearance for the Surrey second eleven, an away match, he made 134 against Northamptonshire. A début century at any level of cricket is of statistical significance and memorable for the century-maker, but when the tyro comes to the wicket with the score at 23 for five and has 65 against his name when the opener who has batted through to that point is later run out for 39, he demonstrates a maturity and a shouldering of responsibility that can bode only well for the future. Although benefiting from a fielding or possibly umpiring error, according to a newspaper report in the scrapbook, he seems to have played an otherwise chanceless innings which clearly made an impression on the Northampton faithful:

> When the hoisting of the 190 took place, Hayes had made 90, the result of some very pretty cricket. Eales bowled from Kingston's end and that bowler should have been credited with Hayes' wicket for a catch in the slips, the first mistake yet made during his innings.
>
> Hayes, who had been at the wicket for about three and a half hours, hit two 5s, eleven 4s, seven 3s and seventeen 2s and with the exception of the above mistake, played faultless cricket, and he was heartily applauded on reaching the Pavilion.

Innings of 41, 38, 21 and 97 followed, prompting C.W.Alcock to write in *Cricket* at the end of the season:

> The Honor Oak C.C., so far as one can judge, seems to have this year furnished to Surrey cricket one of the most promising young players who have combined to produce such a brilliant record for the county's second team. The young cricketer in question is E.G.Hayes, and I shall be much surprised if next season does not find him established in Surrey's first eleven. . . . As Hayes is just twenty, and is, besides, an excellent field

and fair change bowler, there is every promise of a good future for him.

The *South London Mail* was similarly complimentary, though concentrated more on his technical attributes:

> As a batsman Hayes combines steadiness with plenty of hitting power. One special hit is to leg, a really clever, and to many batsmen, an impossible stroke. His two favourite strokes are an off drive and the above-mentioned leg speciality. . . . Bowling fairly fast, he varies his pace with capital judgment, has a slow ball with an off or leg break. . . . In the field he shines best in the slips or the 'country'.

> This short sketch of Hayes' brief but brilliant career, will speedily give my readers an estimate of his superb cricket qualities. Apparently there is only one road which he is destined for and that is the Surrey county eleven and fame and distinction. For so young a player, his powers have been rapidly developed, and mark my words if South London will not shortly be congratulating itself on the entry of one of their players into first class cricket.

Hayes himself saw the 1895 season as being the foundation of his first-class cricket career and was delighted with the welcome he received from the county club:

> This being the season of my engagement with Surrey County Cricket Club of course I naturally look upon it as the start of my cricket career. Having once fully emerged as you might say I was soon successful and made several good scores for both Colts and Club and Ground so much so that a trial match was given me for the Surrey 2nd XI against Northamptonshire and I managed to signalize my appearance by scoring 134 when everything was going against us.

> The 2nd XI were good enough to present me with a silver pencil case on this occasion as a memento, Bob Henderson making a very kind speech when it was given me at dinner the next evening. I shall not forget this kindly welcome into the ranks as it were. Playing in the remaining fixtures I was again successful in most of them . . . so had every reason to be satisfied with my first season with Surrey County.

In all cricket that summer, Hayes scored 2,035 runs at an average of 48.45. As well as his century at Northampton, he had 125 for the county's Colts side against the Non-Commissioned Officers and four further three-figure scores for Honor Oak. Add to that about a dozen innings over 40 and it is not difficult to understand his satisfaction and eager anticipation of the following season as he settled down to a winter job in the Surrey offices. He commented in his scrapbook: 'After . . . my first season's really hard cricket and entrance into the professional world, I well remember how anxiously and with what pleasant thoughts I wanted to try my luck the following season passing the winter in the office of the S.C.C.C. helping Mr Alcock with his secretarial work.'

A first-class début could not be far distant.

Surrey's Second XI in 1895,
including Hayes (back row, left), L.C.Braund (middle row, second from right) and
W.S.Lees (on the ground, left).

Chapter Two
Surrey Pro

we'll talk with them too / Who loses, and who wins; who's in,
who's out
Shakespeare, *King Lear*

Surrey: 1896

That first first-class match was brought closer on 20 May 1896 at
The Oval when, batting at No.3, Hayes scored Honor Oak's first
double century, 210 not out in a total of 313 for two against Surrey
Colts' 273 all out. Honor Oak's innings occupied just 140 minutes,
the first wicket falling at 31, so Hayes was scoring in excess of a
hundred runs per hour.

The *Daily Chronicle* suggested that some of promising youngsters,
like 'Mr' Crawford, Joshua Lohmann, Thompson and Smith might
be tried against Oxford University in The Parks. Particular
reference was made to Hayes, a 'young player who featured in the
'Next Seventeen' match' and who 'seems to have a speciality for
making centuries'. In the event, Thompson played, though he had
first appeared a couple of years earlier in 1894, Crawford and
Smith made their débuts in the return match at The Oval and
Joshua Lohmann never made it, for reasons that were mostly to do
with the strained relationship between the club and his more
famous older brother.

Hayes, however, had to wait until almost the end of the season,
stepping on to the field as a member of the first eleven when his
now long-overdue first-class début came against the Australians at
The Oval on Monday 17 August 1896, exactly one week after the
match in which England had beaten the same team on the same
ground to 'retain The Ashes'. Not that the media or contemporary
reference books attached any significance to that. Indeed it does
not get a mention, the importance of that four-inch urn being
imposed retrospectively on those early Anglo-Australian fixtures.

More significant in cricket's social history than the result, however, though suppressed subsequently in *Wisden* and *James Lillywhite's Cricketers' Annual*, were the events which preceded the Test and dominated the press in its early stages. Four Surrey professionals – Bobby Abel, Tom Hayward, George Lohmann and Tom Richardson – along with William Gunn of Nottinghamshire – had challenged the establishment in the form of the Surrey Committee by 'demanding' a fee of £20 rather than £10 for appearing in the match. Their case was incontrovertible. The fee had been at the same level for nigh on twenty years, international cricket was attracting huge crowds and the Australians were being paid considerably more, as were the amateurs in the form of 'expenses'. The committee, however, was having none of it. What was at the time, and subsequently, referred to as the 'strike' was in industrial relations terms nearer a lock-out. The rebels were replaced. Abel, Hayward and Richardson subsequently backed down, but Lohmann and Gunn held out. Two years later, however, the fee was doubled. The battle had been lost, but the war had been won.

In none of this was the young Ernie Hayes remotely involved, but it was part of the ethos of the Surrey dressing room he joined. His dressing room did not include amateurs Mr W.W.Read and Mr K.J. Key, who would have their own more luxurious accommodation to go with titles and initials on the scorecard, not just their surnames as would Hayes and his fellow professionals. From the start, he would be aware of the amateur-professional divide which was to characterise the first-class game throughout the whole of his playing career and indeed nine years beyond his death well into the following century.

The match itself petered out into a fairly uninteresting draw, but Hayes, batting at five, distinguished himself with an almost chanceless 62 and three catches and was clearly not overawed at finding Abel, Hayward and Richardson among his team-mates and Ernie Jones, Trumble, McKibbin, Giffen and Harry Trott in the opposition.

The frustration at not making the first eleven earlier comes through in the annotations to his scrapbook, though he derives obvious and justifiable satisfaction from his performance against the tourists. For the second eleven, he scored 57 not out against Northamptonshire, 44 against Lancashire, 47 against Hertfordshire and 109 against Bedfordshire. He writes:

These performances at last made the Surrey Committee think of trying me for the County side; and above all matches the 'trial' was against the Australians who were in England this season. Bob Abel and Tom Hayward made a long stand for a start but at last my turn came and having managed to stop a very fast 'yorker' first ball from Jones I played more confidently and managed to score 62. Of course I was delighted with myself and more so when the members in the Pavilion made a collection and presented me with just on £11.

The purveyor of Hayes' first ball in first-class cricket was of course the same Ernie Jones who is the subject of an earlier biography in this series and who once famously put a ball through W.G.Grace's beard, followed up by 'Sorry, doctor, she slipped.'

The media were duly appreciative. The *Standard* bracketed the débutant with internationals Abel and Hayward, reporting that the trio had between them contributed 217 of Surrey's total of 295 and commented further as follows:

The Surrey eleven was identical to that which defeated Kent by ten wickets on Friday last, except that Holland was displaced by Hayes. The latter is a tall well-built young fellow who has made a lot of runs this year for Surrey's Second Eleven. He can bowl, too, but after his success yesterday it is as a batsman that he will be known. He was making his *début* as far as first-class cricket is concerned and both he and his friends have every reason to be proud of the success thereof. Batting from the outset with any amount of confidence, and making some really brilliant cuts and drives, he created an impression which is sure to lead to his inclusion in one or two, at least, of Surrey's remaining fixtures. For two and a half hours he defied the Australian attack and was the subject of quite a demonstration at the close of his innings. ... Hayes ... offered a sharp chance to Trumble at slip when 61. The let off availed the batsman nothing, however, for with a single added to his account, he was easily taken at point by Trott. The ball was one which most batsmen would have left alone, but it would be hypercritical to quarrel with the judgment shown by the colt. Although he made one or two weak strokes, the only distinct chance was the one he offered just before he was out. To make 62 on the first appearance in a big match is not given to many cricketers and the next few performances of Hayes will be watched with more than ordinary interest. He yesterday hit seven fours, a three and three twos.

The Times gave his innings almost two hundred words, said his innings lasted 150 minutes and he 'secured general admiration' from a crowd of 14,000. Hayes mentions in the scrapbook that, after this significant innings, he was sought after by the media for interviews and journalists took the opportunity to comment not only on his batting ability, but also his character and personality. He notes one, for example: 'Personally, Hayes is described as being, like most true sportsmen, a delightful fellow, genial and unassuming with a keen interest in all things affecting the game of which he is already a master.'

Just as any Australian batsman who began his year with some promise in the second half of the twentieth century could be guaranteed that somewhere in the media he would be dubbed a 'new Bradman', so – albeit in a lower key – Hayes was compared to quality contemporary or recently retired players, 'another rising Holland and Hayward' said one and according to Charles Alcock in his official club history, 'a not unworthy successor of Maurice Read.'

However, the 'more than ordinary interest' with which the *Standard* predicted his next few innings would be watched was to be rewarded only with disappointment. After the Australia match, he was selected for Surrey's four remaining Championship matches. A battling 38, against Lancashire on a sticky wicket, was followed by five innings in which double figures were reached on just one occasion when his 29 not out against Somerset was the highest score in the innings. After his promising start, the youngster was in the process of adjusting to the higher standards demanded by the first-class game, though in mitigation, it may be said that all these matches were on sticky wickets. So were many of his matches for Honor Oak, but professional bowlers were able to exploit such conditions in a way that the usually less talented amateurs were not. It was doubtless some consolation to Hayes, however, that, during this rough patch with the bat, he took his first first-class wicket, that of L.C.H.Palairet of Somerset whom he clean bowled in the one over he was allowed.

Wisden was suitably impressed with the newcomer: 'Late in the season a place was found for Hayes, and of this young batsman, who had been doing big things for the second eleven, a great deal may be hoped. In the return match with the Australians – his début in first-class cricket – he played a masterly innings.'

1897

Queen Victoria's Diamond Jubilee year was the apogee of the British Empire and a time of national celebration, but for Ernest Hayes a time of increasing frustration as he found himself thwarted by not being selected for the county side. He writes:

> This season I was very disappointed as I was only played in three county matches and one against Oxford University. Yet I was in very good form and always did well when played. For the whole of the first part of the season I was travelling about with the County team as reserve man. Then I played with the 2nd XI for the rest of the season: chief scores for them being 98, 52, 42, 41, 32 and 73. This being a very useful innings as it was a very sticky wicket v Northampton with the game against us.

He then records his scores in the three first eleven matches in which he did play – 50 and 0 against Somerset; 34 against Kent and 21; and 3 against Hampshire. (He also scored 5 and 0 against Oxford University, but doesn't mention this match!) It would be easy to berate the young professional with a lack of modesty, but it must be recalled that the scrapbooks were never kept with a view to publication, but for his own private use and possibly that of his family. There is no reason to doubt, therefore, that these were his genuine and sincerely held beliefs.

There were two factors which militated against his regular selection. Firstly, it has to be recalled that the county's batting line-up was strong at the time, including Abel, Hayward and W.W.Read and secondly, the prevailing custom – indeed, committee policy – was not necessarily to play the best team, but to give the amateurs first refusal. Gloucestershire's team at the time was mainly amateur (at least notionally), Nottinghamshire's was mainly professional, but for Surrey, who mixed gentlemen and players in their squads[2], there was no doubt who had priority with the backing of a committee of which one-third had titles other than

---

2   A public statement made by Lord Alverstone, the club's president, sets out the county's approach: 'Desirable though it is that the county should always be at the front of county cricket, I certainly do not consider that the county championship should be the only object. I should like, if possible, to arrange matters so that at least three places in the eleven in all county matches should be filled by amateurs.'

a simple 'Esq.' Surrey had a large staff of professionals: their amateurs were mostly batsmen, so that Hayes was placed in a particularly difficult position. Despite their policy, Surrey finished second in the Championship, largely on the back of professional bowling, especially Tom Richardson who took 238 wickets. Surrey won more matches than any other county.

Wisden, without going so far as to criticise Surrey's selection policy, shared the young professional's frustration:

> With a view to strengthening the amateur element in the eleven the Surrey Committee at the beginning of the season gave regular places to Mr H.B.Chinnery and Mr H.D.G.Leveson-Gower. This policy, though we would be the last to find fault with it, told heavily against the young professionals, notably Holland, Hayes and Braund. Not one of these cricketers had anything like a full opportunity of doing himself justice.

However, Surrey's loss was Honor Oak's gain and Hayes continued to fill his boots in club cricket, scoring 124 not out against Battersea, opening the innings and successfully chasing 212 for 6 declared – having been left an hour and twenty minutes to win – and 145 against Alleyn, a match in which he also took six wickets. It was some consolation that this was his best season so far as a bowler and he records with some pride: 'I was pleased to get more wickets this season than in previous ones; obtaining 67 at an average of 9 runs apiece. So, altogether, I think I deserved a more regular place in the county side this season.'

1898

Neither Chinnery nor Leveson Gower, who had been preferred to professionals in 1897, played in the Championship matches for Surrey. Hayes did, though, play in thirteen first-class matches for the county, though without any regularity; he usually batted about eight in the order. However, the frustration increased, as failing yet again to secure a regular first eleven place, Hayes, now 21, wrote in his scrapbook: 'Again at the start of the season I was left out of the County side and felt very strongly the way they were treating me, and feel now that it affected my cricket for a time.'

A couple of half-centuries for the second eleven, against Northumberland and Northamptonshire persuaded the selectors to give him further opportunities with the senior side, but conditions seemed to be against him. He notes in his scrapbook: 'This brought the season to mid-June & I was chosen for the County v Lancashire, having to go in and bat at 6 o'clock in a bad light and only getting 7. Then v Oxford University 5, although I managed to get 4 of the best wickets. It was a funny thing this year that, whenever I played for the 1st XI, I had to go in at about 6 o'clock in a funny light.'

An innings of 35 not out on a 'sticky' against Middlesex followed, then a couple of undistinguished performances meant that he was again dropped to the second eleven before reappearing against Hampshire. On this occasion, he managed to survive the 'funny' evening light and was able to continue his innings the following morning, receiving some complimentary comments from the press:

> The brightest partnership of the day was the first. Abel who had been respited from the overnight trials, opened the ball with Hayes, and the youngster began scoring with delightful zest and freedom. In one over he rapped off ten runs and hit all round with such vigor [sic] that we began to look forward to a century. But when the score stood at 74 he was neatly caught by Lee off Tate. His 38 was knocked off in about three-quarters of an hour and served as a welcome promise for the future. I should like to see Hayes make a lot of runs for he possesses a most attractive style of batting. There is plenty of grace and easiness to his methods and in these degenerate days when care is exercised almost to weariness we can well afford to have a batsman amongst us who is willing to hit out without fear.

However, he remained on the margins of the first eleven and his selection was up and down like a lift in a Peckham tower block. It was with some jaundice in his pen that he wrote: 'The following match, v Middlesex at Lord's, I was sent up to play, but Mr Key decided that Smith should play. I went back to the Oval where the 2nd XI were playing Durham and scored 113 & 20 on a sticky wicket. I may add Smith did not get many wickets (2 I think) & the match was lost v Middlesex, for want of a batsman to stay just 10 minutes to save the game.'

Notwithstanding, his century at The Oval gained him the plaudits of the press: 'Hayes and Lees, whose partnership of an hour added an invaluable 105 for the third wicket. Hayes reached his century in two hours and a quarter and when he was finally caught in the country his excellent 113 included one 6, two 5s, thirteen 4s, four 3s and eight 2s.'

The innings earned him a recall to the first eleven for the Sussex match at The Oval. Although he again made insignificant contributions with the bat, on what he calls a 'perfect pitch' – Hayes is not alone in the reporting of his own cricket, that he does his batting on stickies and his bowling on shirt-fronts – he won the match for his team with the first five wicket return in his first-class career, five for 22. The *Daily Mail* and *Morning Leader* both headlined his match-winning performance, and the *The Times* said that Hayes 'with his slow leg-breaks, bowled magnificently.' Earlier in his career the *South London Mail* reported his bowling 'fairly fast', but this method had by now almost disappeared.

One of the Sunday papers reported: 'The excellent bowling of Hayes towards the end of the Sussex match on Saturday afternoon must have greatly pleased the captain, K.J.Key who, I believe, takes a keen interest in his cricket. That Hayes is going to develop into a good all-round player for his county seems manifest from his recent form. As a batsman he was full of promise, and almost assured of his position in the team.'

The *Pall Mall Gazette* was similarly complimentary: 'Then the game came to an end in a startlingly rapid fashion, Hayes taking the last four wickets; at 229 Butt and Tate were both caught and bowled; and at 231 Humphreys was caught at short-leg, Surrey winning the match at twenty-five minutes past four by 73 runs. Hayes had a remarkable analysis, five wickets falling to him in thirteen overs at a cost of only 22 runs.'

And the Surrey poet, Albert Craig, whose poetry at times makes McGonagall look like Tennyson, supplied the appropriate verse:

Good Old Surrey

And shall I close without a word of praise
To Surrey's future Hayward, Ernie Hayes.
Modest in action in each word and look,
How well he did the work he undertook . . .

C.B.Fry had little doubt about Hayes' potential, writing in his *Book of Cricket*:

The Surrey Club has for some years past pursued a wise and provident policy with regard to its young cricketers. Every opportunity is given to the colts of the county to show their form and, if there is any good promise therein, to improve it. The result is that the Surrey authorities can always fill up vacancies in their First Eleven and know exactly where to look for what they require. Among the young professionals who have come to the front under the judicious system there has been no more conspicuous success than Hayes. He played some time in the Second Eleven. When he got his trial for the county it was evident that his prolific scoring in minor cricket was the result of good form. He has played some fine innings and is likely to prove a very valuable member of The Oval side. He is a free enterprising bat, hitting hard on the off side. He has a tendency to slash rather more than is consistent with safe cricket, but his natural eye saves him from disaster. He hits hard from the bowler round to cover-point and can cut well. There is little doubt that he will improve into a leading batsman. He is a useful bowler of slow stuff on the leg-stump with plenty of men in the country. He is a fine slip. The Oval has great hopes of him.

As in the previous season, failure to be selected regularly for Surrey meant more opportunities to dominate in club cricket. Hayes proceeded to demonstrate that his abilities had progressed way beyond that level with innings of 202, including 13 sixes and 21 fours, against West Kent Wanderers at Blackheath; 129 not out against the London Rifle Brigade and also a 'seven for' in the same match; and 131 not out against Clapton. For Honor Oak that season he had 531 runs at an average of 75.85 and 38 wickets at 5.05. It is a useful rule-of-thumb in measuring the contribution of an all-rounder to look at the ratio of batting average to the bowling average. A ratio of one is a useful benchmark; two is very good; anything better than that outstanding, but 15, like the likelihood of Macbeth's being king 'stands not within the prospect of belief'.

Then, in October, he accepted an invitation to spend the winter in South Africa, coaching and playing for the Standard Cricket Club at Cradock, a small town in the Eastern Cape, about 120 miles north of Port Elizabeth. It was to prove an enjoyable and invaluable experience.

Chapter Three
Coaching in South Africa and then a County Stalwart

'one of the big players of the immediate future'

South Africa: 1898/99

Notwithstanding almost permanent political turbulence in South Africa from the Boer Wars through apartheid and beyond, there has always been a healthy symbiosis between South African cricket and English professionals. For the former, particularly in the nineteenth century, there was a huge advantage to be gained in learning from the experience of those from the 'mother country' and for the latter the opportunity of escaping an English winter, enhancing their earnings and benefiting from contact with a different culture and social structure. George Lohmann is the best known and had a significant influence on early South African cricket, but to his name can be added those of Fred Holland, Alfred Street and now, Ernest Hayes.

Previous tours of English teams, all privately arranged at this time, had been undertaken by Major R.G.Warton in 1888/89, Edwin Ash in 1891/92, Lord Hawke in 1895/96 in the immediate aftermath of the Jameson Raid and Lord Hawke again this same season, as South Africa moved inevitably and inexorably towards the Second Boer War. Some of these tours were of commercial intent rather than with the idea of raising the standard of South African cricket.

The scrapbook annotations reveal Hayes as a man and a young one at that, whose interests extended beyond the tunnel vision of cricket and its immediate hinterland, as he describes the island of Madeira, the one stop on the way to Cape Town, his three days in that city and the majesty of Table Mountain. When he later arrives in Port Elizabeth, he is less impressed by the surrounding countryside which he describes as 'deserted and barren in appearance'. He comments that 'The Cradock cricket ground is bare of turf and drought conditions prevail.' In the twenty-first century, we have become accustomed to 'gap years', but a trip of this kind at this time shows a considerable degree of independence and self-reliance.

Apartheid was already in place. It was not called that at the time, nor was it formalised in the way it was in the post-1948 Nationalist government, but racial segregation already existed as a product of British imperialism. Hayes takes an interest in the Kaffir location and dances and while there is no condescension in an observation that some of the natives play the game very well, he accepts as perfectly natural that they have a club of their own, the 'Rosebuds'. Integration was not on the agenda.

In a later interview, he tells a tale of how an impromptu game of cricket occasioned by a delayed train, arouses the interest of the natives. 'So we got our bats and a ball and played cricket on the veldt, with a crowd of about a hundred Kaffirs standing up in cattle-trucks watching us and cheering every hit.' He adds 'These Kaffirs were placed in cattletrucks like herrings in a barrel and had no room to sit down.'

The cricket writer and historian W.A.Bettesworth, who was conducting the interview, asked whether Hayes had anything to do with the Kaffirs. Hayes replied: 'Not in the way of coaching. At Cradock they are very keen on the game, and know the rules like a first-class cricketer; two or three of them could speak English. They gave the English a good game. They all behaved exceedingly well to me, and took a great interest in my doings and my cricket things.'

He was alive to the cultural differences, as illustrated in the following tale: 'I remember once splitting a rubber handle while practising and throwing it down. Instantly there was a rush of Kaffirs from behind the net to get hold of it. I noticed afterwards that pieces of it were tied on several different bats, and I think they must have regarded it as a species of charm.'

He seems, however, to have integrated pretty well with those of his own colour and culture, taking the opportunity to visit his playing colleagues and opponents of the summer who were in Lord Hawke's touring side and commenting on the poor state of health of his fellow Surrey professional George Lohmann.

His efforts at Cradock seem to have been appreciated. On the eve of his departure a smoking concert was held in his honour at which he was presented with a 'purse and contents'. The local newspaper reported that 'Mr Hayes in response regretted the fact that he was no orator but would compromise by giving another song, at the same time assuring the company present that he was very grateful to the people of Cradock for the kindness extended to him during his stay among them.'

The cricket ground at Cradock, Eastern Cape, 'bare of turf', in Hayes' time.
Note the umpire's parasol.

His coaching duties had not been extensive, working from 4.30 to 6.00 daily with a club he reckoned to be the equivalent of a second-class London one, though with decidedly inferior practice facilities. His own playing performances seem to have been highly satisfactory: playing mostly for the Standard club, he scored 485 runs at 40.41, with a highest of 161 not out, and took 73 wickets at 5.06.

Surrey: 1899

At last the years of spasmodic appearances and erratic selection were over and this year Hayes, now 22, was able to settle down to regular cricket with the Surrey first eleven. He writes with some satisfaction: 'Feeling thoroughly strong and well after my recent South African trip, I started this season with every confidence in myself and can record by far my most successful season up to this time.'

Once again, the Australians were in England and once again Hayes was to make an impression for his county against the tourists, registering the first of his 48 first-class centuries. With the exception of Hayes, Surrey struggled against the accurate medium-pace of William Howell and Hugh Trumble. A press-cutting in the scrapbook records:

> Some of the Surrey batsmen played like innocent children against [Howell's] slow ball, scraping forward in a feeble way and finding themselves utterly deceived in the pace. In the second innings Trumble divided honours with him, the only Surrey batsman who showed any capacity to cope with the splendid bowling being Hayes. This young cricketer who seems now to have fairly secured the place in the Surrey team which ought to have been his two years ago proved to demonstrate that Howell's bowling could be hit with a confidence that was curiously lacking in the efforts of his more experienced colleagues. He is in first-rate form just now, and if he can go through the season as he has begun he will soon be a special pet with the Oval crowd. He seems to have gained considerably in power since last season. ... He strikes one as being one of the big players of the immediate future.

In the first match in May, he had 43 out of 64 in 90 minutes in the second innings as Surrey were annihilated by an innings and 71 runs, never recovering from the devastation of Howell's first-innings return of 23.2-14-28-10. It was virtually a single-handed demolition, eight of his wickets being bowled and one caught and bowled. Hayes then had influenza and was laid up for a week, but had recovered by July and the return match with the tourists when he was to record his maiden first-class century.

Inevitably, Albert Craig produced the appropriate verses:

> Will Ernie prove another Walter Read:
> One hundred 'notches' in the hour of need,
> Cautious, unhurried, patient, watchful, cool,
> Rear'd in Old Surrey's nursery, Surrey's school.
>
> Oh! how his leaders glory in his 'fire'.
> Young Hayes, like Abel, never seemed to tire.

His gallant rivals opened wide their eyes,
Their worthy chief seem'd taken by surprise.

Untiring Trumble, brilliant from the start,
Kept struggling on nor even once lost heart.
Illustrious Noble brought his skill to bear,
Still Ernie kept his post and settled there.

Worrall and Laver grac'd the bowlers track
And yearn'd in vain to see the batsman's back,
At last the well earned century appears.
The Australians join our people in their cheers.

Brave youth to thee our heartfelt thanks we give,
In history's page thy deathless deed shall live,
A worthier pen than mine may write of thee
And hand thy fame down to posterity
But none more gladden'd at the event can be,
And more grateful than thy friend A.C.

Hayes had, almost single-handedly, turned a losing position (Surrey were 53 behind on the first innings) into a comfortable victory notwithstanding Trumble's eight for 35 and five for 137. The ball with a silver-mounted band was presented to him and became a family heirloom.

He reached 1,000 first-class runs in a season, the first time he had achieved this milestone, but it was one he would not fail to repeat before the First World War brought a halt to the first-class game fifteen years later.

Wisden appreciated his value to the county, commenting that 'Apart from Abel, Hayward and Jephson, the batting strength of the side was represented by Hayes, Lockwood, Brockwell, Crawford, Lees, and in a lesser degree, Holland. Of these half-dozen players, Hayes can show the best record, and taking one day with another, he was perhaps the best bat, his fearless hitting being often of the utmost value.'

His season was thus one of considerable success. He batted mostly at three or four, far higher than previously, filling in the spaces left by Frank Crawford, who injured his knee in early June, and Holland also played only rarely in 1899, but had played 21 matches in 1898. He scored his first first-class century in July, off the Australian touring side, before 15,000 people: according to *The Times* it was an innings of 'vigour.' In the Championship he was Surrey's leading catcher in the field, with 24 dismissals, in a team whose fielding was thought by *The Times* to be very good. He was awarded his cap. Although now a first team regular, he also played in a couple of second eleven matches in the Minor Counties championship, now that first-class counties were permitted to enter their second teams in that competition. Perhaps his appearances in the seconds reminded him that his place in the first team was not altogether secure.

Surrey won the Championship that year for the first time since 1895, a remarkable achievement, according to Anthony Meredith in *The Demon and the Lobster*, given internal dissension and the end-of-season resignation of captain, Kingsmill Key. The reason for his relinquishing the office was his disenchantment with the committee's publicly-stated policy of playing as many amateurs as possible. The decision to pay the professionals their match fee when they were omitted to make way for an amateur did little to dilute the resulting disharmony. Against Kent, Key was instructed to play a young amateur, Hugh Dolbey in place of one of the six professionals – Abel, Brockwell, Hayward, Hayes, Lockwood and Lees. All six were or would eventually be Test cricketers. Dolbey was a useful club cricketer. In the event, all six professionals played, Dolbey's sole Championship appearance being earlier in the season against Middlesex at Lord's. The main thrust of Meredith's comments appears to be correct, but on no occasion do any of the 'big six' appear to have been omitted to play Dolbey. Or perhaps Key just chose to disregard the instructions. The committee needed him more than he needed the committee. At any rate, he never played for Surrey again after the end of the 1899 season. And Surrey won the Championship only once in the next half-century.

One remarkable match that summer was the one in which Surrey scored 811 against Somerset at The Oval, eventually winning by an innings and 379 runs. Abel batted through the innings for 357 not out, his score and the team's both still club records.

Hayes' contribution was a modest 56 in a second-wicket partnership of 99.

1900

Now something of a local celebrity, Hayes was invited to distribute the shields and medals for the South London Auxiliary Sunday School Union Cricket Association, on 3 March.

The season began on Easter Monday with a fixture against W.G.Grace's London County, formed the previous year. It was, said Hayes, 'like playing in winter' and was probably very little different in most of the subsequent seasons in which he represented his county against the short-lived first-class side in what were usually back-to-back home and away fixtures which preceded the more competitive matches in the County Championship.

Without Key, Surrey fell to seventh in the Championship, despite winning only one fewer match than in 1899: Hayes played regularly again, batting mostly at No.3, behind Abel and Brockwell, easily reaching the thousand runs milestone in Championship matches, but his bowling was scarcely called upon.

He recorded his first century in a Championship fixture – 150 against Worcestershire at The Oval. His second-wicket partnership of 272 with Bobby Abel set a new county record for this wicket. Abel eventually accumulated 221, and Lockwood 104 not out in a total of 495 for five declared. No one else reached even double figures and the eclipse of Hayward, who scored just five, was a cartoonist's delight.

The *Sun* was cautiously optimistic about Hayes' future prospects. It reported:

> That there is a big career before him is rather more than likely. That he has any amount of pluck he proved in 1896 when an unknown man, so to speak, he compiled an innings of 62 for Surrey against the Australians. At the time the youngster was rather inclined to suffer from that dreadful complaint known as a 'swelled head', but constant association with Surrey professionals (about the most level-headed lot in the country) and further experience has quite cured him of the tendency. There is not the variety about his cricket that one associates with Abel or Hayward, but his driving is very hard and clean.

It is not easy to justify the accusation of conceit. Certainly the scrapbooks show evidence of self-confidence and resentment at non-selection in the early years, but that is some way from having an exaggerated idea of one's own ability implied by

A cartoonist's response to Hayes' first Championship century, 150 against Worcestershire at The Oval in May, 1900.
Abel scored 221, Lockwood 104* and Hayward only five.

swollen-headedness. There are also honest appraisals of the talents of others which would not normally be associated with an egocentric approach and critics in his later years were, in complete contradiction to what is said here, to comment, on Hayes' modesty and complete absence of swollen-headedness. His end-of-season comment, that he was 'completely satisfied with my season's work it being the best I have had until now', is born of neither complacency nor conceit, but of a realistic professional assessment of his contribution to the side. Given his 175 from a team total of 315 against Hampshire at Bournemouth and his 1,248 runs at an average of 32.00, the self-appraisal is no exaggeration.

1901

Census night found him at the Olive Branch Hotel at 27 Sillwood Street, Brighton. He was accompanied by Thomas Dickason, his regular opening partner at Honor Oak a few years before, perhaps enjoying a bit of week-end pre-season training. His father and eldest brother had remained in the area of the drapery trade, the

33

former now described as a 'Manager (Ladies' Underclothes)' and the latter a 'Millinery Warehouseman'.

For Surrey, the season was a disappointment. They won only seven Championship matches, finishing sixth in the table: they failed to record a win in their last thirteen matches. Hayes didn't reach a thousand runs in the Championship, putting him a street behind Abel and Hayward who both reached 2,000. Despite his aggression, he was perhaps a run of the mill county pro in the competition, with 959 runs at 25.23. One game was abandoned without a ball bowled – his colleague Bill Lockwood's benefit match against Yorkshire on 25, 26 and 27 July. A replacement fixture was organised outside the championship for mid-September: Hayes would have cause to remember this later in his career.

His aggressive approach to batting, nevertheless, continued to impress. One press cutting reports, 'Hayes is the type of young man in a hurry, and he has neither the strength nor inclination to play a slow game.' He twice scored a hundred runs before lunch on the opening day of a match, exactly 100 against Oxford University at The Oval at the end of June, and 108 against Leicestershire in early September. It was something of a mixed season. He had a pair against Lancashire; later, against Kent, he scored 0 and 1, stumped by his erstwhile Honor Oak colleague, Fred Huish, in the first innings and bowled by Colin Blythe in the second. By contrast, however, he recorded three centuries; his highest, 121, was in the Oxford match when he shared a partnership of 162 with Fred Holland.

Until now critical comment from the press had tended to concentrate on Hayes' batting and occasional bowling skills, but he was a regular in the slips, taking five catches in an innings in the season's opener against London County, and attracted the plaudits of C.B.Fry, an astute observer of the game as well as an outstanding practitioner. He writes in the *Daily Express*: 'The Surrey fast bowlers are lucky to have such an accomplished short-slip as Hayes, a strong rival of R.E.Foster for premiership in that position.'

Demonstrating another dimension to his talents, he acted as umpire against Cambridge University at Fenner's, for the first and only time in a first-class match. Hayes was 24 and his colleague Bob Carpenter was over 70, a curious contrast, at the time perhaps a record-breaking one.[3] It was Surrey's practice at about this time to have their younger players stand in lesser first-class matches, odd as it may seem to us now. He played in a couple of Minor Counties matches, also fulfilling his obligations as a younger professional. In August, against Devon at The Oval, when Holland took his place in the first team at Taunton, he scored 123, opening the batting in the second innings to set up a successful declaration.

A regular county player, his appearances in club cricket were now rare. Unlike Julius Caesar (the original one, not the Surrey cricketer of the same name), he did not – at least in Brutus' interpretation – scorn the base degrees by which he did ascend and he played for Honor Oak when he was available to do so, often with devastating effect. In that season, he batted three times and scored a century in two of his innings. Against Townley Park, he played virtually a single-wicket match, being last out for 111 out of a total of 170. He then took seven for 49, bowling through the innings to dismiss his opponents for a team total identical to his individual score.

1902

The summer was a wet one and consequently batting performances generally were not as good as in previous seasons. In the Championship overall, wickets came at over five runs cheaper than in 1901: 22.10 as against 27.55. Hayes' own Championship return, 885 runs at 24.58, mostly from No.3, still suggests a run of the mill practitioner. However, he continued to attract complimentary press reports for his style of batting. His one century, 114, that year came against Middlesex at Lord's and occupied just two hours. One of his press cuttings reports that 'There are too many of the careful, plodding style of batsman in the Surrey team at present, and a man like Hayes at the wicket is always a pleasant relief. He and Crawford are the only two batsmen who can stir the Surrey crowd.'

---

3   The age difference between Hayes and Carpenter was 45 years, 354 days. The only instance of a higher disparity in English first-class cricket known to Philip Bailey at CricketArchive occurred at Eastbourne in 1932, in the match Sussex v South Americans, when the age gap between Arthur Millward and Dick Richards was 50 years, 68 days. Strangely enough, Surrey arranged for W.S.Lees to stand in Surrey's home match against Cambridge later in the 1901 season; the age difference between him and Carpenter, who stood in this match as well, was 45 years 37 days. There are no other English matches where the gap has exceeded forty years. Aficionados of this type of abstruse item should note, though, that the birth dates of many less well-known umpires have yet to be recorded by the game's statisticians.

As for his fielding, the press comments: 'Trumper was grandly caught at short slip by Hayes off Hayward, the fieldsman falling on his chest to make the catch.' And 'Hill was run out from a magnificent return by Hayes. The left-hander had late cut Richardson and met his end going for a second run.' In the Championship he took 31 catches: of fielders, only John Tunnicliffe, with 32, took more.

Still playing occasional club cricket, Hayes again turned in an outstanding one-man performance for Honor Oak in a two-day match against Folkestone, following 72 and 201 not out with eight second-innings wickets in a 211-run win.

1903

The season was altogether a better one for Hayes; but it was another wet summer. He remarks, 'This season, although we had bad wickets nearly all the time, proved to be by far the best I had up till then for I finished top of the Surrey county averages and came out top of the catching list for all England.'

He had 1,865 first-class runs at 34.53, including three hundreds and eleven fifties and the press were in agreement with his self-assessment of the season. His slip fielding, where he took most of his 41 catches, continued to attract admiring comments: 'Hayes has been in great form in his position at first slip this season, and though he is not a Lohmann he is about as safe a man as we have at present.'

Wisden commented on the way he had increased the range of his strokes. The 'lack of variety' of three years earlier had now been superseded by the addition of the cut and the leg-side 'draw'. One cutting says, 'Always a powerful driver, he ... greatly improved the variety of his strokes, and was unquestionably the most dangerous batsman on the side. He also fielded admirably at slip.'

After his 145 against Lancashire, the press reported: 'This is distinctly his year. He is batting wonderfully well and can be regarded as the new Maurice Read. ... What I liked about his batting was the versatility of his strokes. A big hitter cannot afford to get all his runs in one direction. Hayes drove hard, he cut hard, but he also cut the late ones with perfect repose, and none of his strokes were so impressive as the draw to leg, executed with splendid judgment.' *Wisden* later reported this innings as 'a superb display.'

He was invited to play for W.G.Grace's London County against Leicestershire. He made a modest 30, but over the season his form had been such that he was a serious candidate for the 1903/04 tour of Australia. However, despite his own aspirations and support from the media, he was not eventually selected. Immediately after the Hampshire match at Portsmouth in late July, he writes in his scrapbook, 'Just about this time a team was being picked for Australia by the MCC. I had not been asked and although well in the running was not asked at the finish.'

Even after the announcement of the team there was still some uncertainty about whether some of those invited would accept and the press continued to make the case for Hayes' inclusion:

In the official statement the MCC announced that they had a list of reserves for the Australian trip in case any or all of the players already invited but who had not replied, should decline to go. It is to be hoped that Hayes is one of those on the reserve list. On present form the young Surrey player has no superior among professional batsmen while for dash he has few equals. A batsman with his driving powers should be a great success on the fast Australian wickets.

Hayes has already proved his ability to make runs against Australian bowling. He made his first big score (62) for Surrey *v* Australians, while his first century for Surrey was also made against the Australians. He is a fine field, and has made more catches this season not only than any other slip but than any other fieldsman. He and Braund would be a splendid combination in the slips. Hayes is also a useful change bowler of the leg break type. Warner has publicly expressed such a high opinion of his abilities that, in the event of Tyldesley declining, Hayes is pretty certain of an invitation.

As it turned out, Tyldesley did not decline, but had a reasonably successful tour, playing in all five Tests and making a few good runs at No.3 in a five-match series which England won 3-1. So, Hayes was not invited and was left to contemplate other options for the winter.

Before that, however, there was a round of charity matches to raise funds for various hospitals at which the Surrey players had the opportunity to demonstrate their social skills as well as their cricketing ones. One reporter comments:

> The Surrey team are not only famous as cricketers but on the society side. Brockwell has a home and colonial for good luck, and 'Tina' Hayes, with his taut moustache, is also first favourite with the ladies, and quite the Adonis of the Oval. Tom Richardson supplies the manly type of fiery beauty, and then 'Glassy' Osborne and Charlie Mills are of the robust style, Henry Clodes the statuesque face . . .

However, on cricket matters, the press in general were critical of the selectors for overlooking the pride of Honor Oak. He played for the Players against the Gentlemen at Hastings and for the Rest of England *v* Middlesex, the champion county, at The Oval, his first representative matches: he was one of only four in the 'Rest' side not to be included in MCC's tour to Australia.

Chapter Four
Overseas Trips and Chaos at The Oval

The heart turns to travel . . .
Ezra Pound, *The Seafarer*

South Africa again: 1903/04

Omitted from the MCC team to tour Australia, Hayes nevertheless decided to avoid the English winter by taking a long sea voyage by the east coast route to South Africa. He had friends in Cradock from five years earlier, family in Durban and his elder brother Arthur had fallen in the Boer War. He returned home via the west coast route thereby enjoying what he subsequently regarded as a 'grand five months holiday'.

Cricket was not on the original agenda, but such was his enthusiasm for the game that he could not spend time in a cricket-playing country without managing to play in a few matches. However, before all that, there was the thrill of the voyage and excitement at spending time in places of historical and geographical interest such as Antwerp, the Bay of Biscay, Lisbon, the Rock of Gibraltar, the Bay of Naples, the ruins of Pompeii, Stromboli, Port Said, the Suez Canal, Port of Suez, Aden, Kilindini, Mombasa, Tanga, the island of Zanzibar, and Dar es Salaam. With the last-named he was less than impressed: 'It is very dirty as a whole the streets being no wider than a passage. Plenty of bazaars selling cheap jewellery, curios &c. Any amount of dirty looking niggers about and the place seems very smelly.'

An articulate and educated man, he demonstrates his ability to think outside the box of cricket with intelligent comments on most of the places he visits. He was, however, inevitably conditioned by early twentieth-century *zeitgeist*. It was the high noon of an Empire on which the sun had at this point in history shown no sign of setting and Hayes was able to write in the full spirit of British imperialism: 'In the harbour area are two British gunboats just to remind the Sultan that we are his boss.'

After Mozambique, Chinde, Beira and Lourenço Marques, the German-owned vessel arrived at Durban, where Hayes left the ship. After visiting his brother Arthur's grave in Pietermaritzburg, he continued his holiday with his friend Charlie Barton, at the isolated settlement of Nottingham Road, about seventy miles inland from Durban. He wrote:

> Here there is only the hotel & a store or two. Farms lay all around at various distances. Supposed to be one of the healthiest spots in Natal. Xmas Day we spent very quietly. We had a knockabout with a cricket ball in the morning and had a splendid Dinner, as near a Xmas Dinner as it was possible to get out here: included Turkey and Xmas Pudding. While here we were nearly every day to be out on horseback. Had some splendid rides over the hills. They have a fine polo team here and I saw them play a match at Mooi River which they won easily.

In Durban while visiting his cousins, he met some of the local cricketers and joined the Wanderers Cricket Club. League matches were played over two Saturdays and consequently he was only able to play one of those, making 75 not out and four, but he did join a team styling itself the Nomads which went on a tour through the battlefields in the western part of Natal. Playing surfaces were less than immaculate. One ground, Hayes reports, had been used for camping and was consequently very rough. He finds some interest in places still showing traces of the ravages of the war, such as Ladysmith:

> . . . we passed Glencoe and other places where the war had been. Had a good look round Ladysmith and found it most interesting. The town hall has still its broken clock tower and two shells were embedded in the walls. The Royal Hotel too has great holes made by shells right thro' the ceilings and walls. Hills surround the place & it is indeed wonderful how our soldiers held out so long, for the shelling must have been terrible . . .

> Leaving here as early as possible the train took us over Colenso Bridge, which had been broken down by the Boers and rebuilt by our people, also through Chievely the scene of Buller's Camp, past the hill where the Boer guns were placed & which

the British rushed, also the graves which lay here and there all over the place. Just a little pile of stones and a wooden cross. Passing also just before dark where Long's guns were captured.

He moved on to Mooi River, one of the last places the war reached in Natal. The camp was still there and those still in occupation provided the opposition for two days of cricket. On the first, Hayes made 55 and took four wickets against the Royal Artillery and the next against the 7th Dragoons, had 188 and seven wickets.

It was then back to Nottingham Road, followed by a month in Durban with his cousins, before returning, this time by the west coast route, on the *Armidale*, having clearly enjoyed his winter away, excited by travel and taking a keen interest in the significance of recent historic events.

Surrey: 1904

Refreshed by a winter overseas, which had provided him with some cricket, though that had not been the purpose of the trip and it had been no sort of practice for the first-class game, Hayes reported to The Oval. Convention demanded an amateur captain. The club was unable to find one to do the job on a regular basis, with the result that a poor, rudderless season saw Surrey lose twelve matches out of 28 – a figure exceeded only once since – and finish in eleventh place in the County Championship. The palmy days of the previous decade and the successes under John Shuter and Kingsmill Key were almost a distant memory. There were wider problems, too: they fielded 34 players in the competition, and were now without the bowling strength of Lockwood and Richardson for most of the season.

Hayes had a mixed season – he was, though, Surrey's leading batsman in the Championship. The absence of success on the northern tour – 'I have never done well on this tour,' he laments – was counterbalanced by a couple of fifties against Essex and a career best at the time of 273 not out, his first double century in first-class cricket, at Derby, taking part in three century partnerships on the way. It was a far from chanceless innings, but occupied only five and a half hours and included a six, a five and 39 fours. It was later to be eclipsed as the highest innings of the season by Percy Perrin's 343 for Essex, also against the hapless Derbyshire. Without Bill Bestwick to open the bowling, Derbyshire captain A.E.Lawton had no answer to Surrey's and Hayes' dominance. In a letter to the *Daily Mail* he wrote: 'We haven't won today; we didn't even make a draw; we just lost. Had we played another three or four days, we should probably never have got Hayes out.'

Wisden had no hesitation in placing Hayes second only to Hayward in batting quality and the *Cricket Star* commented: 'He is one of the most popular men Surrey ever played, not even excepting Abel or Lohmann or Shuter and in the Honor Oak district they speak of him with awe.'

Earlier in the season, he had enjoyed some success as a bowler, taking six for 48 against Derbyshire. A reader of the *Cricket Star* put it in context:

> In taking six Derbyshire wickets for 48 runs, E.Hayes accomplished the finest performance of the week. When it is considered that the match produced nearly 1,000 runs, that Lockwood's ten wickets in the match cost over 170 and Lees's one wicket 150 runs, the value of Hayes's bowling will be seen. Among his six victims too were C.A.Ollivierre and Storer, so they were by no means a batch of poor wickets.

He caused some amusement at Leyton:

> Cases of absent-mindedness are not unknown among cricketers, and Hayes did not create a record when, on his turn coming to go the wicket, he walked out of the pavilion at Leyton without his bat. But the spectators were naturally delighted when they saw his look of bewilderment on discovering that he had forgotten something of importance.

Later in the season, at Beckenham, a lady spectator, said to be the wife of R.N.R.Blaker, the Kent amateur, had a lucky escape:

> . . . Hayes made a fine on-drive and the ball fell on a lady who was sitting in the tea pavilion. The lady might have been seriously hurt but the ball happened to drop on her watch and, although the watch was completely smashed its wearer was unharmed.

In the third week of July[4], he added 102 runs to his overnight score before lunch on the second day of Surrey's home match with Yorkshire off, among others, Rhodes and Hirst. There is a press cutting in the scrapbook, on which he does not comment, to the effect that, 'the bowling was far superior to that which yielded the slim Surreyite his [then] record, 273 not out at Derby,' and 'while sacrificing nothing of his characteristic dash, he was always playing good, sound cricket, which lost nothing in attractiveness from the unwonted restraint.'

It was, however, a sad summer for Hayes in that his mother died, having been unwell for some time. As a result he missed the match against Sussex at Brighton, towards the end of July.

West Indies with Lord Brackley: 1905

For the early part of 1905, Hayes was able to secure himself two separate but related jobs, firstly as one of two professionals (the other being George Thompson of Northamptonshire, who had begun his career as an amateur) on Lord Brackley's tour of the West Indies[5] and secondly as correspondent for *The Sportsman* on that tour. He summarised it all as 'a glorious trip some of the islands being perfectly lovely.' The side comprised thirteen players in all; they took with them John Moss of Nottinghamshire, as

---

4   Earlier in July, appearing for the Players against the Gentlemen in a high scoring game, he stumped J.H.Hunt for 128 off the bowling of Sam Hargreave, when the professionals' captain, Dick Lilley handed him the gloves in the latter stages of the amateurs' innings. He took one other stumping in his career, off Len Braund in Western Australia in 1907/08, when he shared the wicketkeeping duties with his captain A.O.Jones in the last match of MCC's tour.

5   Lord Brackley (Hon John Francis Granville Scrope Egerton), who was aged 32 at the start of the tour, was the eldest son of the third Earl of Ellesmere. *Wisden* gave him only four lines of obituary, but his career reads so like a parody of an Edwardian sporting aristo, that it deserves to be better known. He was educated at Eton, but seems not to have been in the Eleven. His only first-class match before this tour was for MCC against Nottinghamshire at Lord's in 1898, a rain-affected match in which only 21 overs were delivered, all on the first day, when he neither batted nor bowled. Usually reported as a middle-order batsman, his batting average in twelve first-class matches between 1898 and 1905 was 14.00. Shortly after returning from the tour he married Lady Violet Lambton, the eldest daughter of the fourth Earl of Durham. He was appointed MVO in 1909, an honour in the personal gift of the sovereign. He served as an officer in the Scots Guards in the Boer War and the Great War. He was MCC president in 1920 and later a senior steward of the Jockey Club, being a well-known racehorse owner of his day. He succeeded his father as fourth Earl in 1914, inheriting country estates at Brackley in Northamptonshire and in Berwickshire, and industrial estates in Lancashire and Cheshire with collieries, coke works and wharves. The family owned a house in Bayswater, with a picture gallery which included several Raphaels, Titians and Rembrandts. This was damaged twice by enemy action in 1941, but many of the pictures had been removed elsewhere. When he died in 1944, he was succeeded by his son who was in a German prisoner-of-war camp at the time.

umpire and G.Bellamy, as scorer. They had arranged to play twenty-one matches of varying durations, some against odds, spread over almost three months from 12 January to 6 April. Ten of these matches are now treated as first-class. The players seem to have been chosen for their social qualities: some no doubt chose themselves. Only Hayes and H.V.H.Hesketh-Prichard had played more than a dozen first-class games in the 1904 English season. None of them, including Hayes, were anywhere near the top twenty in the season's batting and bowling averages.

He was obliged to seek permission from Surrey to join the tour. It was granted readily enough – by the Secretary and confirmed by the Committee – albeit with the rider that, following the precedent of Hayward and Strudwick in Australia, no winter wages would be paid.

Lord Brackley's well-clad team on their outward journey to Jamaica in December, 1904, aboard S.S. Port Kingston.
Standing (l to r): J.Moss (umpire), G.J.Thompson, E.G.Hayes, T.G.O.Cole, C.H.M.Ebden, G.H.Drummond, S.Beton, G.Bellamy (scorer).
Seated: G.H.T.Simpson-Hayward, A.W.F.Somerset (wk), Lord Brackley (capt), C.P.Foley, E.G.Wynyard, R.C.W.Burn.
H.J.Powys-Keck and H.V.Hesketh-Prichard are absent.

Life on board ship was pleasant enough and although most at some stage suffered from what Hayes delicately called *mal de mer*, there were sports such as quoits and potato races, nets and a cricket match of sorts against the ship's officers. He reports enthusiastically: 'Instead of running we had chalk lines across deck at different distances, hitting the ball over which counted one, two, three or four. Our opponents were not nearly strong enough, and we won by 271 to 51.' Other entertainment was provided on the way out by Mr F.R.Benson's Shakespearean touring company, who acted the balcony scene from *Romeo and Juliet* and a scene from *The School for Scandal*.

Although West Indian cricket at the time was inevitably dominated by white men, as they had the time and the money, the presence of black and Asian players was tolerated – and indeed welcomed – if they were good enough, although club cricket in Trinidad, for example, was segregated by social class and social divisions followed racial lines. The divisions were not, however, as watertight as those experienced by Hayes on his earlier trips to South Africa.

West Indies cricket did not have Test status. There is a reference to cricket being played in the West Indies in *The Pickwick Papers* (1836) and the origins of inter-colonial cricket can be traced back to a match between Barbados and British Guiana on the Garrison Savannah in 1865. There had been a tour to Philadelphia and Canada in 1886 and to England in 1900. English teams had visited the Caribbean from 1894/95 and although the two matches against West Indies on Lord Brackley's trip were designated 'Tests' by the press, West Indies had to wait more than two decades for official Test recognition.

The party landed at Kingston where the weather was delightful, the heat tempered by a cool breeze and although Hayes found the buildings 'old fashioned and disappointing', he was impressed by the 'electric car service' and the 'wild flowers in full blossom, beautiful ferns of all kinds of species, palms and cactus and orange trees full of fruit'.

There can be no doubt that the locals embraced the British-introduced sport of cricket with enthusiasm, though at this stage principally as spectators rather than participants, but with time and a different, cavalier, approach, they would later in the century be the game's greatest exponents.

The natives, who form the majority of the spectators, have caused us much amusement by their enthusiasm, for they closely watch every ball bowled and yell with glee if a four is hit or a wicket falls and when their own side are batting generally shouting out advice to them on how to play . . .

Capt Wynyard and Ebdon opened our innings against the bowling of Morrison and Moiston. The latter is a native and a really good slow leg break bowler. . . . Nelson, another native who was keeping wicket, proved himself throughout the match a really good stumper.

The correspondent of *The Sportsman* was certainly impressed by the standard of cricket he met on the island:

The cricket was certainly much better than we had been led to expect, and they have evidently improved since the last visit of English cricketers. Several of their best players are quite young and there is no reason, if the interest in cricket here is kept up, that in a year or two they should not have a really good team. One more word of praise to them for their fine fielding which all through was quite as good as that of any county side I have seen.

Notwithstanding, the All West Indies side lost the first *soi-disant* Test match by an innings and 17 runs, but gave a better account of themselves in the second, losing a close encounter by just four runs.

The itinerary was intensive – Jamaica, Barbados, St Lucia, Barbados again, Demerara, Barbados for a third time, St Vincent, Trinidad and back to Plymouth. There was also to have been a trip to Grenada, but that was cancelled because of an outbreak of smallpox on the island. The cricket was, however, tempered by picnics and social events, such as dinners with multiple and doubtless seemingly interminable speeches.

As in Jamaica, in Barbados too, local exuberance was unavoidable, though far from unwelcome. He reports: 'The natives were most excited, running all round us when we were leaving the field and shouting expressions of approval. One man took hold of Thompson's arm and kissed it. As we drove back to the hotel, they lined the streets and danced about in a most amusing manner.'

Hayes was to have a century against Barbados, as well as half-a-dozen economical wickets and a further century against

British Guiana where the tropical vegetation and local enthusiasm again created an indelible impression. 'Outside the ground there is a lovely avenue of samoy trees, and the branches were packed with natives, looking like so many monkeys peeping through the leaves.' It was a remark which in other times and circumstances would have brought a severe reprimand and ban of several matches from a match referee, but in the context of early twentieth-century colonialism, it was innocuous enough.

Such is the intensity of present-day tours that players often have little opportunity to see anything beyond grounds, roads and airports. But in a more leisured age, while the amateurs were being entertained at Government House, Hayes and Thompson and perhaps Moss were left to their own devices. They were able to absorb something of the local atmosphere; they took a drive into the country and observed:

> This place is below the level of the sea and they are obliged to have large trenches in nearly every street. Some of them look very pretty the water being covered with lovely lilies. Coming to a little village called Providence[6] we saw a native funeral which was an interesting sight. About a hundred black girls followed the hearse, all being dressed up in pure white with a purple sash around them. ... Coming home, our driver nearly pitched us into one of the trenches, and then the police pulled us up for not having lights, but kindly excused us on finding who we were. So altogether we had a good time.

The personable Hayes was, on this trip and others, an ideal tourist. Despite the social gaps between the professionals and the amateurs, unlike a number of his contemporaries and successors, he was neither a misfit nor a maverick and fitted in to the touring ethos, as demonstrated by the aristocratic exchange of correspondence between the tour manager and Surrey chairman recorded in the club minutes:

---

6   The 'little village called Providence' is, of course, now the site of a modern cricket stadium, one of a number purpose-built for the 2007 World Cup.

Dear Lord Alverstone

Not having the pleasure of knowing personally any of the Surrey Cricket Committee I write to say that E.G.Hayes, who has been one of my team touring in the West Indies for the last three months, has done great work from the first match to the last and a more charming man to have had on a cricket tour I could not have asked for. I hope you will inform the Surrey C.C.C of the above.[7]

Brackley

His tour was a playing success, too. Overall, he was the leading run-scorer, with 925 runs at 38.54, and had the highest innings on the tour, 173 against St Lucia in a two-day game. He was 'the leading all-round man', according to *Wisden*, scoring in nine first-class matches 425 runs, including two centuries, and taking 26 wickets. *Wisden* thought 'his fielding wherever he was placed' was 'superb.'

---

7   No doubt Hayes reported on Lord Brackley's behaviour to his own peers in the Surrey professionals' dressing room.

Chapter Five

Under New Management, Test Cricket, and a Purple Passage

His work bears the hallmark of class whether he is batting,
bowling or fielding.

Surrey: 1905

After the uncertainties of the previous season, 1905 was much
more satisfactory for both Hayes and his county. Stability returned
as Lord Dalmeny filled the previous year's vacuum in the
captaincy: it had originally been the intention that Dalmeny would
give way to J.E.Raphael in July, but he was so successful that the
arrangement was not carried out. Surrey finished fourth in the
Championship, winning fourteen of their 28 fixtures.

Hayes wrote of himself:

> This proved to be a most satisfactory season for not only did
> our team do much better but I was in good form with both bat
> and ball and was chosen for Players *v* Gents at Lord's and the
> Oval, the Players *v* Gents of the South at Hastings and for the
> rest of England *v* Champion County at the Oval. Before the end
> of the season, I also received an invite to join the MCC team in
> South Africa during the winter months and accepted.

His assessment of his own performances was shared by the media
who confirmed his status as an all-rounder. The following
appeared on the heels of an innings against Warwickshire when he
was bowled for 99 by one which turned 'out of the rough':

> Another Surrey cricketer of the indomitable type came within
> an ace of making a century in the same innings, namely Ernest
> Hayes. It is rather difficult to name a more typical all-round
> cricketer than Hayes. I doubt indeed if any other player can do

as much as he can in all departments of the game. His batting has two methods though he does not love purely defensive tactics; he can bowl in two styles; he can field, catch, run and throw in as well as, if not better than, any other player now before the public. And he is a trier of triers. There are younger men in the Surrey XI, as well as a contemporary or two who can afford to take a lesson from him in this respect. Hayes is, it seems, likely to be at his best this season and more extraordinary things might happen than his inclusion in an All England XI.

Earlier in his innings at the end of the first day's play, he had been similarly praised: 'Hayes was to the fore both with the bat and the ball. He is the Surrey all round man at the moment. Four wickets for 46 and 43 not out is not a bad day's work.'

All was going swimmingly and furthermore, some strengthening of the county's batting line-up was on the horizon in the form of 'the promising young Cambridgeshire professional who has qualified for Surrey and may revive her past glories.' Although Jack Hobbs was never quite able to do that – it is bowlers who win matches and, consequently, Championships – he was, with the other two Hs, Hayward and Hayes, to form a batting trio that was to dominate many a county fixture and, off the field, be translated into a lifelong friendship.

Hayes had a distinguished performance against Worcestershire:

The dashing Surrey batsman has rarely been seen to better advantage than at Worcester on Saturday. He came in at a most critical period when Surrey, with nine wickets to fall, required 189 to save the innings defeat on a pitch that had been ruined by rain, and on which the Worcester bowlers were carrying all before them. By free and fearless hitting, Hayes speedily demoralised the bowlers, and in the course of an hour all fear of a Surrey defeat had practically been dispelled. Hayes made his first 50 in fifty minutes, and though he did not maintain this rate, it is beyond dispute that he knocked the bowlers off their length and saved the game for his side. All the circumstances being considered, his 152, not out, was perhaps the best innings he has ever played. It was quite free from fault and was characterised by daring driving. His timing was a marvel of accuracy . . .

He was Surrey's leading scorer in the Championship, with 1,616 runs at 39.41 in 27 matches. His successful performances were not restricted to county cricket: for the Players at Lord's, his first time in this fixture, he drove and pulled his way to 73. He cannot have been far from Test selection against the Australian tourists: the No.3 position went to J.T.Tyldesley, who was usually followed in the batting order by C.B.Fry and F.S.Jackson, so the competition was formidable.

By no stretch of the imagination could Hayes be classed as an all-rounder in the accepted sense of one who can command a place in a side for the discipline of either batting or bowling (competence in the field being understood), but he came closest that season to being what in modern parlance would be called a 'batting all-rounder'. Playing in 36 first-class matches, he bowled more than 500 overs and took 76 wickets at 23.30, including a 'five for' and 'six for' in consecutive matches at the end of May.

South Africa: 1905/06

For the third time in his life, Ernest Hayes was to spend a winter in South Africa. This time, though, it was not as a club cricket coach or holiday tourist, but as a member of the first MCC side to tour there, under the captaincy of Pelham Warner. The latter had been there before as a member of Lord Hawke's team in 1898/99, so both Hayes and his captain had the advantage of familiarity with the territory. Not that it seems to have done either of them any good. From the cricket point of view, Hayes had a regrettable and forgettable trip, South Africa had her first Test victory and went on to win the series 4-1.

Unfortunately, Hayes' success in three of the deck sports events (potato race, file and cigarette race, gentlemen's bridge, double deck quoits, bucket quoits and mixed bridge) and an early 125 against a Griqualand West XV were not portents of continued domination on a tour dogged by poor form and ill-health.

Christmas Day was enjoyable enough, spent as the guests of the Mayor and Mayoress of Johannesburg, the First Test at the Wanderers ground in that city which opened the New Year of 1906 rather less so.

Having made 91 in their first innings, the hosts were on the back foot at 105 for six, requiring 284 to win in the fourth. A century partnership turned matters round but, when Test débutant Hayes, the seventh bowler tried, took the eighth wicket, the pendulum had swung back towards England. Then an unbroken last wicket partnership of 48 by Nourse and captain Sherwell took South Africa to a memorable win and concluded a modest and mediocre start to Hayes' undistinguished Test career. Batting at No.5 and coming in at 15 for three after the demise of Warner, Fane and Denton, he had made 20 in the first innings, three in the second. He was not alone in failing to impress. *The Sportsman* recorded that, with the exception of Crawford and Haigh (who was primarily a bowler, but had only one over in the match), the batting was 'quite unworthy of the side'.

England players taking the field at the Newlands Ground, Cape Town, probably in the Fourth Test, South Africa v England in March, 1906.

Hayes records that he had a rare run of bad luck, could not do right, was troubled with colds and later at Cape Town, tonsillitis. At Cradock, he had been able to renew acquaintance with some old friends, visited the Congo caves and witnessed diamond mining at

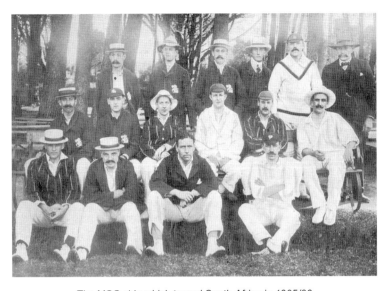

The MCC side which toured South Africa in 1905/06.
Back row (l to r): J.H.Board (wk), C.Blythe, E.G.Hayes, I.D.Difford (manager),
E.G.Wynyard, J.Phillips (umpire).
Middle row: A.E.Relf, J.N.Crawford, H.D.G.Leveson Gower, P.F.Warner (capt),
F.L.Fane, J.C.Hartley.
Front row: W.S.Lees, S.Haigh, L.J.Moon, D.Denton.

Kimberley, but these were exceptional moments of happiness in what turned out to be a miserable trip, both on and off the field.

The weather and travelling did not help. Parts of the country were hot and dusty, having had no rain for eight months. He comments:

> From Oudtshoorn to Johannesburg was now the order and what a journey it was. Three days and three nights in the train and the heat terrific. We all thanked goodness when we reached Jo'burg and could enjoy a bath and general clean up. After a couple of days we were due to play the 2nd Test Match. It was just my luck the day before the fixture while practising to put my finger out of joint and incapacitate myself. Jack Board hit one straight back at me and I tried to catch it.

A rather gentler Jack Board story was related by Hayes in a later newspaper interview when reminiscing about his experiences on the tour:

> Jack Board was keeping wicket when our opponents started their second innings. Just before the first ball went down he

The scoreboard at Albert Park, Durban, at the end of MCC's first innings against Natal on 17 January, 1906.
Hayes' 35, batting at five, was his highest first-class score of the tour.

noticed a fair-sized spider right on top of the off stump. He pointed it out to some of us, but did not disturb it and the innings began. ... When the innings finished, those stumps had never been touched in any way, and the spider had completed its web, which stretched right across the three stumps from off to leg.

So Hayes missed the Second Test which England lost by nine wickets, though he did not begrudge the South Africans their success, judging them to have the better bowling side in their own conditions referring to the 'matting wickets which did not suit any of us too well and the Africans have some fine new bowlers. They are a splendid side on their matting.'

He had recovered sufficiently to be selected for the Third Test, also at The Wanderers, made 35 and 11 not out, but was part of a side which was to lose by 243 runs and hand South Africa an unassailable 3-0 lead in the rubber.

He found a bit of form in the next match, but injury and illness continued to follow him. He remarks tersely: 'Saying goodbye to all our Jo'burg friends we were now off to Bloemfontein and have played XV of Orange River Colony. I came into form this match and scored 66 & 40 about time too. Also sprained ankle.'

The ankle injury was insufficiently serious to keep him out of the Fourth Test match at Newlands, but this time illness was to strike again and he was unable to make any contribution, batting down the order at No.9 and No.7.

> From here to Cape Town for our last two Test matches. In the first one, after fielding on Saturday, I was taken bad. I managed to get there on the Monday for a knock but got a duck. Went home to bed and getting up to have a 2nd innings, got another duck, thus 'bagging' them. We won this match by 4 wkts. In the last Test we were well beaten by an innings and 16. I was ill with tonsillitis and did not play.

He recovered in time to enjoy his last three days in Cape Town. He concludes: 'This finished our tour and we sailed for England on the 'Norman'. I for one being heartily pleased as I had had such an unsuccessful time although thoroughly enjoying myself.'

Wisden's summary of his performances in his eight first-class matches makes particularly dispiriting reading. In spite of his familiarity with local conditions, he scored 186 runs at 14.30, with a top score of only 35. His 32 overs of wrist-spin, an activity where his South African opponents were sometimes close to unplayable, brought him just two wickets for 123 runs.

Hayes 'relaxing' at his cousin's home in Durban, January 1906.

1906

This season will be recalled by statisticians as the year of George Hirst's 'double double' of 2,385 runs and 208 wickets – unique, and given the reduction in the amount of first-class cricket, unlikely ever to be challenged. Ernest Hayes was never going to compete with that, but he did enjoy what was statistically at any rate his most successful season. He achieved his highest run aggregate (2,309) and highest batting average (45.27) and proudly records:

> This turned out to be one of my best seasons up to date and also a real good one for the Surrey team. Under an admirable skipper we made up a lot of lost headway and finished third in the Championship. I was again chosen to represent the Players *v* Gents at Lord's and was once again successful scoring 5 & 55: also chosen for return match at The Oval and final match at Scarborough, in the later scoring 13 and 122 not out.

There were diversions including a trip to Epsom Downs to watch the Derby, the Surrey players taking advantage of the racing connections of their aristocratic captain. They were, however, unable to escape the attention of the press whose members were at this stage beginning to take just a little interest in players' off-field activities:

> The early finish of the Surrey and Gloucestershire match was greatly appreciated by The Oval players, who turned up in great force at the Derby on Wednesday. Lord Dalmeny was with his father, and many players were in the big ring. When the big race was over Ernest Hayes was observed wearing a big buttonhole and a bigger smile, and smoking a cigar that seemed to spell satisfaction.[8]

For Surrey, batsmen dominated; Hayward had 3,518 first-class runs (unsurpassed until Edrich and Compton's 'Brylcreem summer' of 1947), including four consecutive centuries, a feat never beaten for the county and equalled only three times, by Jack Hobbs in 1920 and 1925 and by Ian Ward in 2002. In June, Hayes had a golden nine days in which he scored 218 against Oxford University, 54 against the touring West Indians and 126 against

---

8   The cutting is ruefully annotated to the effect that Hayes lost a 'fiver' on the day.

Cambridge University, going through 1,000 first-class runs for the season in the process.

Firmly established at No.3, Hayes had seven centuries that season and additionally some of his shorter cameos made significant contributions to his team's performance. He followed his half-century in the Lord's Gentlemen *v* Players match in 1905 with another one in pursuit of an unlikely victory target of 300 to give his team an outside chance. Though ultimately in vain, the innings attracted the admiration of *Wisden*'s correspondent: 'When at 54 a blunder in running cost Hayward's wicket the match seemed all over, but Hayes and John Gunn – Hayes playing incomparably the better cricket – brought a change and shortly before half-past three, the Players, with four wickets in hand, only wanted 90 to win.'

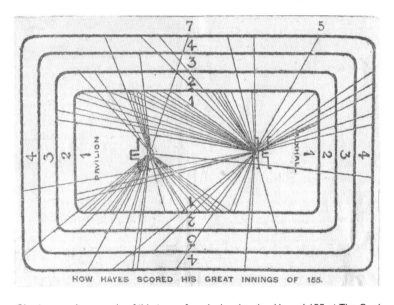

HOW HAYES SCORED HIS GREAT INNINGS OF 155.

Chart, an early example of this type of analysis, showing Hayes' 155 at The Oval against Leicestershire on 10 and 11 May, 1906.
This was the first of his seven first-class centuries this season.

Victories against Yorkshire – the only county with more wins than defeats against Surrey – were always satisfactory, perhaps few more so than that at The Oval in 1906, against the full might of Lord Hawke's team which included Wilfred Rhodes, George Hirst and Schofield Haigh. Hayes played his part in what was a satisfactory benefit match for his friend, Walter Lees:

> No one gave a better exhibition of clever, forceful batting than Ernest Hayes. It was a great pleasure to see this batsman in form. It is worth anybody's money to see him when he gets going. His hitting is so clean, so incisive, so inspiriting [*sic*]. He never half hits a ball. He has the virtue of knowing what he has to do, and he has the ability to do it. Smashing cuts, full-shouldered drives, and clever leg placing, alternated in quick succession. His 53 was a delightful display.

Perhaps the outstanding performance of the season, however, was his batting at Hove. It had been a low-scoring match and Hayes' 97 had been by some distance the highest score of the first three innings. Surrey had been left a none-too-easy target of 198 to win and Hobbs had gone early. Hayes' 105 not out in the second innings ensured a nine-wicket victory.

Interestingly at this stage, Hayes was the dominant partner in the Hayes-Hobbs relationship. One reporter notes, 'Hobbs, in a subdued key, acted as a good foil to Hayes. He was twice as long as Hayes over his runs.' Hobbs was of course at this stage in only the second season of a long and very distinguished career. Hayes was in his eleventh English first-class season, possibly at his peak; but it is nevertheless something of an enigma that Hobbs went on to dominate the game while the story of Hayes, at international level at any rate, remains one of unfulfilled potential.

Hayes finished the season with impressive innings in the Scarborough Festival – 84 for the South against the North and 122 for the Players (his highest in the twelve Gentlemen v Players matches in which he played) and had MCC decided to send a team to Australia that winter, the name of Ernest Hayes would almost certainly have been on the list.

> The inevitable decision not to send a team to Australia next month is unfortunate for Hayes. Known to be a useful player in all three departments of the game for several seasons, Hayes has worked his way now to a certain position in England's Test match team. His work bears the hallmark of class whether he is batting, bowling or fielding, and he is a regular M.R.Jardine[9] in the field, backing up in the most unexpected places, doing the

9   The father of D.R.Jardine.

work of three men at short slip, or wherever else the fortune of the game may place him. Popular among amateur and professional alike, he would today have been among the first six certainties voted for by a selection committee at Lord's, or in the Players dressing room anywhere. Hayes is a good bowler, but whenever he gets wickets there is certain to be surprise expressed. If Hayes goes to Australia in September, 1907, he will not be the worst batting average when the statistical pencils get to work in March 1908.

Though not unreasonable at the time, the forecast in the last sentence was regrettably over-optimistic.

He had 50 catches for Surrey that year (54 in all) which remained a county record until surpassed by Stuart Surridge in 1952.

Off the field his charity work continued and along with Walter Lees, he was elected an Honorary Life Governor of Richmond Hospital, recognising them as 'two of England's best cricketers who have most kindly for many years played in the hospital cricket match.'

Rip's cartoon of 1906 recognised the same skills which were emphasised by Wisden.

The following spring he was nominated one of *Wisden*'s Five Cricketers of the Year along with Surrey amateur colleagues, J.N.Crawford and N.A.Knox. The citation mentioned that he had added the pull to his drive, that his batting was 'lively and adventurous', and that he had no superior among Surrey batsmen except Hayward. Recognising that he had now been associated with Surrey for more than ten years, the Almanack went on to comment that 'Hayes has never yet had the honour of being picked for England against Australia but he would be a credit to a representative team.'

1907

That was to be remedied the following year, however. Surrey, with Lord Dalmeny still at the helm, and Hayes at three following fellow aspirates Hobbs and Hayward, finished fourth in the Championship. Hayes had a good season; he was Surrey's leading run scorer in the competition, with 1,721 runs. With fewer not outs than his rivals, he was third in his county's averages with 37.41, behind Hayward's 46.17 and Hobbs' 40.88.

A 'wonderful week' in August saw 95 and 104 against Nottinghamshire, followed by a double century against Middlesex – an innings quoted by Pelham Warner, who himself made 149 in the match, as one of the best he had seen. In the second innings, Hayes' wicket was taken by the Middlesex fast bowler, Edward Mignon. They were later to share a wife – consecutively, not concurrently.

He was not asked to play in any of the three Test Matches against South Africa, their first in England, that summer, but with all due respect to the tourists, then as now Australia was the 'big one'. Nor did he play in any other 'showcase' match. Despite this, Hayes records: 'This again proved to be a very successful season for me and led to my being asked to join A.O.Jones' Australian team.'

Chapter Six
Failure in Australia, Success at Home

Bouncebackability
Iain Dowie

Australia: 1907/08

The outward journey on the *Ophir* was some way from being the ultimate in luxury. Jack Hobbs, writing almost thirty years later, recalls that it was 'quite inferior to the ships used in the present day for pleasure cruises'. He and Hayes shared a cabin in the forward part of the ship 'where the motion of the vessel could be experienced to the full.'

As in South Africa three winters earlier, the tour was not a successful one for Hayes. He reflects: 'This trip although a most enjoyable one was a very unsuccessful one for me until just on Xmas and then got 98 & 50 in consecutive matches, but afterwards was played but little.'

He added that there was little chance of practice and he never had the opportunity to play his own game. In the first match against Western Australia at Perth, he was lbw for nought, the only such score in an MCC total of 402 which was sufficient to win the match by an innings and 134 runs.

Eight against South Australia and four against Victoria, batting at No.8, was followed by 12 against Queensland and 13 against an Australian XI at Brisbane. He found the heat in Queensland 'terrible', up to 112°F, 44°C. New South Wales he found rather more comfortable where, as other tourists before and since, he thought the Sydney Cricket Ground the finest in the world: 'Wickets, fielding, stand accommodation, banks and dressing rooms all perfection.'

By comparison he was less impressed by Queensland and empathised sufficiently with the following poem to include it in his scrapbook. Banjo Paterson it is not, though the atmospherics are not dissimilar:

The Bushman's Farewell

Queensland, thou art a land of pests
For flies and fleas one never rests
E'n now mosquitoes round me revel
In fact they are the very devil,
Sandflies and hornets just as bad.

Stunted timber, thirsty plains,
Parched up deserts, scanty rains,
Rivers here you can't sail ships on
And nigger women without shifts on,
Humpies, huts and wooden houses
And nigger men who won't wear trousers.

To stay in thee, O land of mutton
I would not give a single button;
But bid thee now a long farewell,
Thou scorching sunburnt land of Hell.

He was unhappy that captain A.O.Jones did not give him a chance in any of the Test matches 'which disappointed me greatly'. In view of his form, he may not have had much of a case for inclusion, but he was the only member of the party not to play in a Test match. His fellow tourist Sydney Barnes, writing to Hayes almost half a century later, took the view that he should have been played and drew a parallel with his own treatment when he was omitted from the England side after a match-winning performance. Be that as it may, his returns in eleven first-class matches of 230 runs at an average 16.42, and five wickets for 193 runs off 46 six-ball overs, tell their own sad story. Even his highest score, 98 before a crowd of 12,000 at Albert Park, Melbourne, against 'A Victorian XI', was later diminished by *Wisden*'s report that 'the match was not played very seriously.'

It was, therefore, a glaring case of unfulfilled potential and while Hayes was honest enough about his own shortcomings, he did not hold back with criticism of selection in other areas, nor of the umpiring. The following post-tour interview appeared in *The Sportsman*, under the heading 'A Chat with Hayes':

Australia has been reckoned the graveyard of many cricketing reputations. Under the burning sun, upon adamantine and terribly fast wickets, in the strange glaring sub-tropical light, Englishmen possessing great names at home have often completely failed to reproduce the form which secured an invitation to make the tour. . . . The ordinary man – he who pays his sixpence at the gate to see part of a county match – will tell you that the MCC tour in Australia in 1907-8 will always be remembered for the loss of four matches out of five, and the comparative failure of Ernest Hayes.

The interviewer recognises that 'Hayes made no bones about it, and fully admitted that he had not got 'going' upon Colonial soil.' He says that 'the umpiring was pretty bad all round, with England the greatest sufferers.' There were, however, compensations: 'A bevy of Fremantle girlies went to see the Brattishers[10] play the soccer game' . . . 'they criticised the good looks of the visitors, unmindful of the play' . . . 'they were unanimous that Hayes was the chief Apollo, with Braund a good second.'

1908: Benefit Year

After the disappointments of the Antipodes, Hayes settled down to another round of county cricket, his tenth season as a regular player, under a new Surrey captain, H.D.G.Leveson Gower. He managed to recover some form, but contended that luck was against him.

However the regard in which he was held in the club is perhaps demonstrated by his top table placing next to the captain at a dinner given for the staff by the club's President, Lord Alverstone:

> Although in a lot better form than during the Australian trip, yet bad luck seemed to pursue me this season & time after time I was out to some marvellous catch. Still having finished up with 1200 odd runs – 33 wickets and also catching 38 out could not grumble overmuch.[11] My benefit match *v* Lancashire was a failure in one way as it rained all three days but luckily I was insured for £1,000 & our people granted me another match, North v South at the end of the season but unfortunately the weather was very cold & after paying expenses, I had again to draw £20 off the Insurance Co, so I might easy say that the insurance people gave me my Cricket benefit.

10   sic – 'Strine' for Britishers
11   He rather underestimated his catches, taking 45 in the season.

The season had started on Easter Monday, 20 April, with Surrey *v* Gentlemen of Surrey, a match said Wisden 'contested in bitterly cold weather' when 'early on Monday morning', The Oval was covered in snow. It must have been quite a shock to the nervous systems of those like Hayes, recently returned from a southern hemisphere summer. He made 56 at No.3 out of a total of 390 as Surrey won by an innings and 41 runs. The low temperature, a maximum of 44°F (7°C) on the opening day, may have contributed to Hobbs and Hayes not staying long at the crease – they failed to make a run between them – and to W.G.Grace's decision to play no more first-class cricket. Now in his sixtieth year, he signed off with 15 and 25.

The match chosen for Hayes' benefit – Lancashire at The Oval – was completely washed out, with not a ball bowled on any of the three days. It coincided with the Olympic Games athletic events at the White City, so the choice of dates may have been a little unwise. The ground was visited by campaigning suffragettes who were refused entry. Not that there was any cricket for them to watch, but maybe that was not the main purpose of their day out anyway.

Still, what could have been a financial disaster turned out, through Hayes' cautious foresight, to produce a tolerable return in the

Hayes' benefit plight recorded by two cartoonists.

shape of proceeds of £1,264 for a premium of £150. Not all professional cricketers were as astute, a number being left with very little after the deduction of expenses; nor were they as fortunate as some of their amateur brethren. Yorkshire's Lord Hawke had a testimonial in the same year which yielded £1,843.

A collection was made during the Nottinghamshire match in early August which realised £79 3s and a further one during the fixture against Yorkshire, a match in which Hayes deputised as wicket-keeper for the injured Herbert Strudwick and claimed five catches.

The replacement benefit match at The Oval on 10, 11 and 12 September was not an undiluted success, the weather being cool throughout. An attendance of 3,600 on the first day and rather fewer on the second saw the South extend their innings to 501 for 6 declared with J.W.H.T.Douglas, according to *Wisden*, showing a 'degree of caution for which there was no necessity whatsoever.' Hayes had made 66, Hayward 112. Several big names were occupied elsewhere in the Hambedon *v* England celebrations at Broadhalfpenny Down and Leveson Gower withdrew from the South at the last minute. The North managed 293 and 154 to lose by an innings and 54 runs. Hayes chipped in at the end with one for 17. Surrey retained most of the funds he had raised and invested them for him, a rather paternalistic approach which was common at the time and which continued in some counties until the 1950s.

Earlier that year at Headingley, against the bowling of principally Hirst and Haigh, he outscored all his colleagues combined with a fifty he regarded as one of his best innings, saying in an interview with *Cricket* which appeared on the day of his benefit that 'a 30 or 40 is sometimes a better and more useful innings than 150'. That was probably an untypical effort though, perhaps as a result of his performances (or, more accurately, non-performances) of the previous winter, his style was beginning to attract some criticism, albeit of a positive and constructive kind.

The *Sporting Life* had this to say:

> Even in the face of gratuitous advice from his critics to play himself in before forcing the pace, he has gone on hitting hard and early. He has realised that the gods designed him specially to attack, and that has been the foundation of his successful career.

The harshest criticism levelled against his batting is that he begins to hit before he has got his eye in. We hear a great deal about this when a batsman fails at what he is best at. When W.W.Read got out through attempting the pull shot, he was told that the pull was spoiling his game. When 'Ranji' got out lbw through attempting to leg-glance, we hear sermons on the folly of the stroke. And yet every batsman must get out some time, and he is generally attempting some kind of stroke when beaten. When Hayes flicks at the first off ball and retires caught at slip, his lack of restraint is made much of.

But let him get his first off ball past third man for four, pull-drive the next two from the middle stump to the long-on boundary, and go on getting 'em for the next hour or two, and his early hitting is not called lack of restraint. It is called brilliant forcing cricket, and other batsmen are recommended to try the same methods instead of taking half a day to play themselves in.

Hayes is an audacious batsman and sometimes he pays for his audacity. He sometimes makes his shots at balls as wide as to invite disaster: he oft-times attempts to hit straight good length balls to square-leg and there is more than a suspicion of slash about his game.

There is nothing very polished about his strokes. His drives do not flow in rhythmical curves. They are sheer blows quick and sudden. He is seldom guilty of the forward push strokes . . . he does not worry about his average.

He might not have worried about his average, but he was certainly aware of it, recording it faithfully in his scrapbook in most seasons, along with details of his centuries, but the question must be asked as to how a man so successful at county level was a relative failure on the international scene. It is a question that has been asked of others, in more recent times, perhaps most memorably Graeme Hick and Mark Ramprakash, and some of the answers may be the same.

For a start there is the question of temperament, though there is nothing to suggest that Hayes was prone to 'freeze' or was a victim of stage-fright. He certainly was unlucky with injuries and illness in South Africa in 1904/05 and was never given an opportunity in Australia in 1907/08. Newcomers rarely shine in a losing side and the teams he accompanied to the southern hemisphere were certainly that against the emerging strength of South Africa and an Australian team which did not particularly impress Hayes, but was still good enough to win four Tests out of five. The most likely explanation – and there are hints in the *Sporting Life* feature – is that he failed to adapt to the different, slower tempo of Test cricket, the longer time scale contrasting with the relative urgency of three-day cricket.

The criticism of attempting to play attacking cricket before getting one's eye in is one which a hundred years later has been levelled at Hayes's successors in the Surrey line-up. Alistair Brown, Scott Newman and James Benning spring to mind. None has been given the opportunity to play Test cricket, so it is impossible to say how they might have adjusted. Yet the psychological approach to Test cricket has shifted in recent years and the belligerent attacking game of Jayasuriya, Gilchrist or Dhoni contrasts markedly with the grind-it-out earlier approach of Bannerman, Barrington or Boycott. Perhaps Ernest Hayes was a man ahead of his time. How he would have relished the challenges of limited overs cricket, especially Twenty20.

Albert Craig, the Surrey rhymester, collecting for Hayes' benefit at The Oval. Craig helped many beneficiaries in this way.

1909

This year was an outstanding one for Hayes. Once again he was on the top table at Lord Alverstone's dinner, but this time had to sing for his supper – quite literally – with renderings of '*Two Eyes of Grey*' and '*Would You Care?*' The former seems to have been his party-piece which he sang at a number of functions along with '*Somewhere*' and '*Look Down, dear Eyes*', all long-forgotten turn-of-the-century ballads and obtainable, if at all, only through antiquarian booksellers.

His on-the-field entertainment was, however, somewhat more memorable. He records with some pride:

> This was by far the most successful season I have had for some years. Right from the start I did well and eventually finished up with the highest aggregate and also the highest individual score in England. And this season also I reached the height of a cricketer's ambition, that is to play for England in a Test Match. I also played in both Gents *v* Players matches. During the season I had the honour of acting as captain of Surrey on three occasions.

His captaincy of Surrey, albeit in an acting capacity, represented a rare challenge to the social structure and reflects the high regard in which he was held by his county. The highest individual score to which he refers was his 276 in a county total of 742 against Hampshire, also his career-best, an achievement of some distinction, though not quite the distinction it was claimed to be by a Northamptonshire newspaper which mis-printed the scorecard, recording it as 476 and hailing a new world record.

His partnership of 371 with Hobbs, who also made a double-century, was genuine and remains the record for Surrey's second wicket. Its duration was 2 hours 45 minutes, part of what was at the time another record of 645 runs for four wickets in a five hour day and the first time a Surrey innings contained two separate double centuries. The match was eventually won by an innings and 468 which was then and is still the county's second largest margin of victory.

For Hayes, however, there was a downside. Hobbs takes up the story.

A short time before when we were due to play a match against Northamptonshire, a certain gentleman, unknown to me, brought a bat to The Oval and said, 'If you will use this bat in the coming match and score a century with it, I will give you a five-pound note.' I agreed; the same offer was made to Ernie Hayes and accepted. We both failed in the Northamptonshire match and, when the gentleman made the same offer for the match against Hampshire, I was willing to try again, but Ernie thought that the bat was responsible for his poor score on the previous occasion and would not take on the proposal. Well, I scored the 205 with it, and the strange visitor presented me with ten pounds. Ernie was terribly vexed; he had actually beaten my big score on that day and hit up a splendid 276. That self same type of bat became known as the 'Force' bat; it was placed on the market and is a good seller.

Notwithstanding that, Hayes was able to mitigate his failure to cash in by endorsing the bat he had used. Later that year an advertisement proclaimed 'the highest score by Hayes and the biggest hit by Mr J.N.Crawford were made with Stuart Surridge's PRD[12] bats.'

At Northampton, he carried Surrey to a narrow two-wicket victory, scoring 144 not out from a winning total of 242 for eight. The next highest score was 37 and, having shared an unbroken ninth wicket partnership of 29 with Herbert Strudwick, he perhaps paused to reflect on the progress his career had made since his century on the same ground on his Second Eleven début fourteen years earlier.

He was part of the Surrey team which beat the Australians by five runs that season and was the first to 2,000 runs, his consistent good form resulting in an invitation to join the England team in the final Test at The Oval. Previewing the match, one newspaper recalled Hayes' first-class début and drew a parallel with his 'first appearance in international cricket'. (In fact, it was not, but 'away' Tests in South Africa were clearly not endowed with the same significance as 'home' ones against Australia.) The cutting reads:

> Ernest George Hayes has a peculiar distinction. Born at Peckham 33 years ago, he attracted attention by his high scores for Honor Oak. His début in first-class cricket was against the

---

12   Patent Rapid Driver.

Australian team of 1896 on the Oval. It is a coincidence that thirteen years afterwards he should be asked to make his first appearance in international cricket on the same enclosure – the Oval that he knows so well. If the man of 33 can match the lad of 19, cricketing England will be delighted.

Of the match, Hayes himself writes:

> Next came the crowning event of my career – that of playing for England *v* Australia. As it happened I was only successful in one department of the game that of fielding, although always in a different position than usual. But fortunately my runs were not wanted the game being a hopeless draw, thus Australia won the rubber winning two matches to England's one.

It was the final Test match of the summer, played at The Oval, and 'The Ashes' although recognised, were by no means as significant as they were subsequently to become. The match was the one in which Frank Woolley made his Test début and also that in which Warren Bardsley became the first batsman to score a century in each innings of a Test match. Hayes had undistinguished innings of four and nine and bowling figures of 4-0-10-0 and 2-0-14-0.

In his only innings for Honor Oak that season, Hayes scored 98 against Bromley Town. Despite being able to make only rare appearances for the club, he never lost touch with his roots, taking a county side to play the club in most seasons, serving on the committee in the first part of the century, then being made a Vice-President and later a Life Member.

The previous season, in an interview with *Cricket* magazine to mark his benefit match, when asked to comment on the possibility of a tour by Australia and the likely outcome of the series, he said:

> I hardly think they will come over, but should they do so we certainly ought to win the rubber for they are by no means as strong as they used to be. The old ones are getting older and the young men are not so good. Why, even with our 'second eleven' side out there last winter we should probably have won three at least of the Test matches had we taken our chances.

In retrospect, both series seem to have been classic cases of English underachievement – by no means the only ones in cricket history.

Surrey's Annual Report was suitably complimentary:

The batting of the eleven was on the whole strong. Hobbs was at the head of the averages in the County Championship matches, being closely followed by Hayward and Hayes. Indeed, Hayes, though third in the order, proved himself a pillar of strength to the side, the manner in which he rose to the occasion, when Hayward and Hobbs were away, being worthy of the highest praise, and provides an example well worthy of the emulation of all our younger players.

Hayes reported that he acted as captain in three Surrey matches in this season. Research has shown that he led the side in only two, though perhaps he may be referring to taking charge in another game, no longer identifiable, when his captain was off the field of play. The two games where he led the side from the start were against Somerset and Sussex at The Oval at the end of July. His sides, which were both all professional, were distinctly depleted, with Hayward, the senior professional, and Hobbs both absent injured and Marshal[13], their talented but disputatious Australian, suspended for indiscipline. Jack Crawford's famous dispute with the Surrey committee over the composition of the side against the Australian tourists on 15-17 July had by then led to his dismissal as deputy to Henry Leveson Gower, the appointed captain, who played only intermittently in this season. Hayes' sides defeated Somerset by an innings, but just hung on to draw with Sussex. During the season Surrey also suspended Lees and Rushby, so that the complimentary tone of the annual report about Hayes may have had rather wider intentions, and was perhaps even tinged with relief.

Four of the Surrey team, Leveson Gower as captain, Strudwick as wicket-keeper, along with M.C.Bird and Hobbs were invited to join the MCC tour to South Africa for the 1909/10 winter. Hayes was not among those selected, but his previous experience meant that his opinions on South African conditions – and politics – were sought. Of the Wanderers, venue for two of the five Test matches, he had this to say:

> Picture to yourself an almost circular playing arena, nearly as big as Kennington Oval with a banked cycle track skirting it. On one side a row of stately eucalyptus trees separates the ground from Park railway station, but not a blade of grass is to be seen.

---

13   David Lemmon's book on Surrey suggests that Marshal was suspended after he and other players were stopped by the police in Sheffield for playing with a child's football in the street and refusing to give their names!

The playing field is a monotonous study of brick red, broken only by the strip of greenish-brown matting spread over the wicket. After a few overs the ball takes on the colour of the outfield, and players unused to these conditions find it difficult, especially if a dusty wind is blowing, to follow its flight.

Such a wicket is the googly expert's paradise, for the ball nips very quickly from the pitch, and men like Faulkner, Vogel, Schwartz and White can effect an abnormal break. The outfield is as true and fast as a billiard table. Surprise is often expressed that a turf wicket has not been laid down in Johannesburg. As the rainy season in the Transvaal coincides with the cricket season, a turf wicket on some occasions would be unfit for play for weeks on end. But the red-brick soil has such marvellous recuperative powers that the ground may be deluged in the morning and be perfectly fit for play three hours later.

Natives are not admitted as spectators to matches at the Wanderers' ground, but at Cape Town, where the MCC men will have a turf wicket provided for them, the black population take a keen interest in the game, and utter weird exclamations of surprise and admiration when Sinclair and Nourse are in hitting mood. In Durban the Indian population are enthusiastic followers of the game. Decked out in their gaudiest habiliments, they squat round in groups and watch every stroke with the closest attention.

Hayes played in 37 first-class matches in this season, the most appearances he made in an English summer. This may therefore be a place to reflect on the life of a busy Surrey professional in the Edwardian era, and the stamina required to support it. Of the 37 matches, all of three days' duration, 31 were for Surrey and six for other sides; three of these were 'big' matches – a Test match at The Oval, Gentlemen versus Players at Lord's in mid-July and the champion county game in September. He played against the Australian tourists five times. His first match started on 3 May and the last, at Bray near Dublin, ended on 20 September. His matches were spread over 21 weeks, and in 16 of those weeks he played in two games. Of the total of 111 possible days' play, he lost nine, either when matches were finished in two days or when a full day was washed out. On the field of play he had 65 innings, 28 of which lasted for an hour or more; he sent down just over 350 six-ball overs in 42 innings, fifteen times bowling ten or more overs in an innings. He played twenty matches at The Oval, and another four elsewhere in London, with thirteen involving travelling from the capital. In June he had three consecutive away games at Bournemouth, Northampton and Horsham: later he had successive matches at Sheffield, Chesterfield and Manchester. All his travel, of course, was by public transport, and overnight accommodation sometimes meant a dodgy bed and breakfast.

1910

In spite of the loss of Crawford, Rushby and Marshal, the season was a successful one for the county, thanks mainly to 'Razor' Smith and his 215 Championship wickets. But it was a disappointing one for Hayes as, after a good start he spent much of it injured, a rupture of the calf muscles causing him to miss nine county matches. Still batting at three, his contribution to the Surrey's second place in the Championship was 1,007 runs at 32.48, a dozen wickets and 35 catches. Now 33, he failed to score a first-class century in the season for the first time since 1898. Nor did he 'trade up' to any of the more important representative matches: the No.3 place there was firmly in the hands of J.T.Tyldesley.

Hayes (left) arriving for practice at The Oval at the start of the 1910 season.

In an interview with the *Cricket Star*, Hayes produces his thoughts on 'bad patches' of the kind which seem to have dogged his brief and intermittent international career 'and recently experienced by David Denton of Yorkshire and Mr J.R.Mason of Kent.' 'It was an interview given in the spring,' he comments ruefully, 'but kept I suppose until I have a queer time myself.' He openly and honestly enters into the psychology of it all and concludes that perhaps too much cricket is being played leading to what in later years would be called 'burn-out'. A hundred years or so down the road, little if anything seems to have been done about it, apart from exacerbation in the wrong direction and the extension of the playing season for international cricketers to twelve months a year. He says:

> A year or two ago I remember I went completely off colour. The lack of success troubled me greatly and like many men in similar circumstances I suppose I got a trifle disappointed and down-hearted. And when a man does that (though there is every excuse for him after a long spell of bad luck in the field) it all tells against any renewal of his olden triumphs, against his driving away the cloud that is surrounding him. For such feelings engender a want of confidence in any man. And when a batsman or bowler, or even a fielder, begins his day at cricket without any confidence in himself, why, he might nearly as well keep off the field all together for all the good he is likely to be to his side.
>
> . . . even unknown to himself there is lurking within him somewhere that slight touch of indisposition which makes all the difference in the world between excellent success and all too frequent failure. Or it may be that he has 'overtrained' so to speak. He has had too much cricket. The exigencies of a long season of stern matches in the County Championship with other struggles wedged in between these, nowadays prove too much for many estimable cricketers. He is generally playing every day and all day from 1 May down to the end of September if he has been a prominent and regular member of a county eleven. Do you wonder that he has his off-days now and then – sometimes many of them too?

Simplistic psychology perhaps, but words that will find an echo in the heart of many a professional sportsman.

1911

The summer was one of the driest on record with virtually no time lost to the weather. Consequently cricket was played on pitches favourable to batsmen and, although Hayes had a reasonable enough season, finishing well behind Hayward in the Surrey averages, in his own judgment he should have done better than an aggregate of 1,597 at an average of 37.13. He had four centuries, his highest 137 not out to save the match against Warwickshire at Edgbaston and 123 against Lancashire, as well as 95 against the All-India touring team. Surrey's fifth position in the Championship was a disappointment, with Warwickshire taking the title for the first time.

His slip-fielding technique continued to impress, with only K.G.MacLeod of Lancashire taking more catches in the Championship: 'Any young beginner might well take the first opportunity he can to watch E.G.Hayes, the Surrey professional. Hayes is on his toes from the time the bowler starts to run and so far as it is possible to anticipate a mishit he does so.'

Still maintaining strong links with the Honor Oak, Hayes captained a Fifteen of Surrey side, against Eighteen of Honor Oak. His side included Tom Hayward, Herbert Strudwick, 'Razor' Smith, John Hitch and Walter Lees, as well as Honor Oak 'old boy', Fred Huish, now of Kent, and replied to the locals' 204 with 369 for 12.

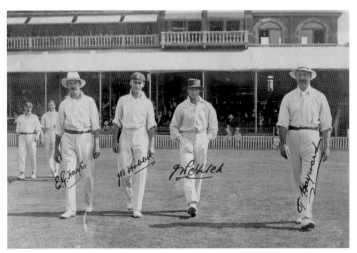

Hayes and his fellow aspirates take the field in interesting headgear at The Oval on one of many sunny days in 1911.

Chapter Seven

The Golden Age Ends on the Western Front

Lions led by donkeys
Max Hoffman

1912

A year in which the loss of the *Titanic* put sport in its proper context was a successful one for Hayes, who had an outstanding season until the weather deteriorated in July and August, but even then he topped the Surrey batting averages by a considerable margin.

Surrey were not doing well, but Hayes was. *Wisden* observed: 'Surrey's batting, apart from Hayes, who played splendidly on all sorts of wickets, was not consistent. ... Hayes ... has never played better. He was in form when he started play at the end of April, and in form he remained until a sprained wrist kept him out of the closing match.'

He was the second batsman – and first English player – to score 1,000 first-class runs and was an almost automatic selection for the Gentlemen *v* Players fixtures.

Against Gloucestershire, he had the best innings and match bowling figures of his career, following a remarkable 17.5-6-22-8 with five for 79 in the second innings, one of two occasions he had a ten-wicket match that year; at Leyton, batting in his usual position of No.3, he carried his bat through the remainder of the innings and was in a Surrey side which again beat the Australians, this time by a margin of 21 runs. Hayes captained an all-professional Surrey team *v* Worcestershire in early May at

Dudley, even though Hayward, the senior professional, was in the side.

The press commented on his consistency. In consecutive innings in the second half of June, he had 143 not out, 90, 38, 40, 117, 37, 16, 85 and 69. Once again, his claims for international selection were advanced:

> Comparisons are odious, but when the recent doings of Hayes are compared with one (if not more) member of the English eleven, it is difficult to understand why he has been ignored so far for the Test matches, and even the trial games. Is it assumed that he does not possess the Test match temperament as it is called?

As suggested earlier, it was probably less a question of temperament than of a combination of batting style and bad luck through illness and injury, but he was eventually given a further opportunity to resurrect his Test career when chosen for three of the Triangular Tournament matches between England, Australia and South Africa. This experimental tournament, itself the brainchild of the infant Imperial Cricket Conference, aroused little interest and has never since been repeated, except in the form of three-way limited overs international competitions.

The ill-fortune which had accompanied his earlier international career again reared its head and he played in only one game, making four in the eighth match against South Africa which England won by ten wickets. He had earlier been omitted from the final selection against Australia at Old Trafford in a match in which the Manchester weather restricted play to five hours and allowed only one innings to be completed. Then he was ruled out of consideration for the deciding match at The Oval when influenza put him out of action for three days.

Promise was again unfulfilled. A local newspaper happily reported the selection: 'The selection of Ernest Hayes will be cordially welcomed and on form the honour has not come a moment too soon. . . . Mr E.G.Hayes, who resides with his friend Mr R.B. Depledge[14] at Whitcomb Lodge, Wellington-road, Hounslow, has once again been honoured . . .' Some houses on Wellington Road, now part of a cosmopolitan area of West London, dominated by

---

14   Depledge was a Tattersalls bookmaker, local Councillor and well known locally as a charity fundraiser.

flights into nearby Heathrow Airport, survive from the period, but Whitcomb Lodge is not one of them, unless it has changed its name or had it removed.

A national newspaper drew a flattering comparison with Ranjitsinhji, under the heading 'Ranji and Hayes':

> Another batsman who is essentially a natural as opposed to a self-constructed cricketer is Hayes who for nearly ten years past has been one of the most under-rated men in England.

> Hayes never has played, and never could play, to the gallery, and the last complaint in the world from which he will suffer is the swollen head. Yet there is practically nothing he cannot do. I have seen Hayes play cricket in England, South Africa and Australia with varying success, yet with only a modicum of failure. He can keep wicket when necessary, bowl in two ways and field anywhere. If I had to have half a dozen men, who were certain not to be passengers in a side, Hayes, Llewellyn and Tarrant would, I think, head my list.

Hayes, now in his thirty-sixth year and aware perhaps that there would be no more international opportunities, reflects ruefully:

> It was at this time the Selectors at last put me among the team to represent England. It was the match against the Australians at Manchester but to everyone's surprise on a very wet wicket they played Hitch a fast bowler and made me reserve. The match was spoiled by rain, play only lasting a little over one day.

> I was again picked to represent England v Africa unfortunately on a sticky wicket and this time played but in a match we won easily I only scored 4.

> The next representative match, v Australians at the Oval, I was again picked but had the hard luck to catch a real bad cold and was laid up for 3 days with influenza.

The fact that Hayes was down on his own luck did not prevent him making notes on the prowess of his fellow professionals. History has shared his judgment of the two he mentions as doing particularly well in this match: 'In the African match Barnes bowled magnificently and Jack Hobbs was grand with the bat.' Hobbs had 68 out of a total of 176 and Barnes bowled unchanged throughout the match with figures of 21-10-28-5 and 16.4-4-29-8, as South Africa failed to reach three figures in either innings.

Hayes played little cricket after that, illness being followed by injury. He did, however, turn out for a combined Surrey and Middlesex side against the Australians. He writes: 'This proved to be my last big match for Surrey for during the match I fell and strained my wrist badly and was unable to handle a bat properly for the remainder of the season, altho' as there were only 11 players at Hastings for the South of England v Australians I played and went in No.8, one handed.'

Again, Hayes was instrumental in a county side playing against Honor Oak at Colyton Road. Hobbs top-scored in a tight draw.

1913

This was an unexceptional year, summarised by Hayes as follows: 'Although this was a good dry season I did not come up to my previous years form but could not grumble as I scored 1,300 odd runs & took 30 odd wickets.' All his matches were for Surrey and he played in no representative matches.

For Hayes' colleague, Tom Hayward, however, the year was not unexceptional. He recorded his hundredth century, joining W.G.Grace as, at that stage, the second entry on that particular page of the record book. Led by M.C.Bird, in his third season as captain, Surrey finished third in the Championship: Hayes had now, though, to compare himself with Hobbs, who scored 2,238 runs at 52.04 in county matches.

The third of the four Hayes scrapbooks concludes with some notes on his philosophy of the game and a plea for what was later in the century called 'brighter cricket' in the way of aggressive batting, attacking bowling and improved fielding. Also required are better spectator facilities; and he mentions the importance as a public relations exercise –although it was not, of course, referred to in those terms – of the work of now deceased 'Surrey poet', Albert Craig.

1914

For Surrey it was a good year, but the events of August put cricket into perspective. Hayes writes laconically: 'War with Germany being declared in August caused the season's cricket to finish hurriedly, but nearly all the programme had been gone through and Surrey were returned CHAMPION COUNTY. Injuries kept me out of the team for a few matches in August.'

Before that, however, in early May, he had produced an invaluable all round performance in the match against Somerset. Headed 'The Value of Hayes A Splendid Victory', it reads:

> Ernest Hayes carried off nearly all the laurels at Kennington Oval yesterday when thanks largely to his superb all round cricket, Surrey beat the clock by an hour and a half and, incidentally, Somerset by 241 runs. Possessing a lead of 207 runs with eight wickets in hand [The two out were Hayward for 5 and Hobbs for 0], the home county entered upon the concluding stage of the match with a commanding advantage, but still it was necessary to score quickly in order to declare as early as possible. Here it was that Hayes played a great game for his side and after he had knocked up 99 out of 166 runs added in an hour and 25 minutes, Surrey found themselves in a position to apply the closure before lunch. Hayes played a magnificent innings, occupying two hours and a half . . . his 129 included fourteen 4's, three 3's and sixteen 2's.

Somerset were left 374 to win. Then

> . . . directly Wilkinson introduced Hayes to the attack at the pavilion end the game steadily went against the visitors. Hayes soon disposed of Braund and Daniel. . . . Somerset were all out in two hours and a half for 132 runs – a poor performance. . . . Hayes five wickets cost less than seven runs each, so that he has every reason to feel proud of yesterday's work.

His final figures were 14-4-34-5.

Two centuries against Yorkshire, one at Bradford and one at Lord's (whither Surrey had transferred three home fixtures later in the season, as The Oval had been requisitioned by the War Office) demonstrated a liking for White Rose bowling. In the same innings, Hobbs had 202, Hayward 116, the only occasion on which the trio all reached three figures in the same innings. Surrey declared at 549 for 6 and eventually won by an innings and 30 runs.

Foreshadowing things to come in the next decade, Hayes umpired again – a match between the second elevens of Leicestershire and Warwickshire at Park Road, Loughborough. It was one of a number

One Penny.

Surrey County Cricket Club.

KENNINGTON OVAL.

SURREY v. GLOUCESTERSHIRE.

MONDAY, AUGUST 31, 1914.   (Three-Day Match.)

SURREY.	First Innings.		Second Innings.
1 Hayward	c Board, b Ellis	1	....
2 Hobbs	c Smith, b Toogood	141	....
3 Hayes	lbw., b Toogood	50	....
4 Mr. D. J. Knight	c Sub., b Toogood	102	....
5 Harrison	b Toogood	8	....
6 Mr. C. T. A. Wilkinson...	c Champain, b Parker	14	....
7 Mr. P. G. H. Fender	b Parker	0	....
8 Abel (W. J.)	c Ellis, b Toogood	52	....
9 Hitch	b Parker	17	....
10 Strudwick	lbw., b Toogood	0	....
11 Rushby	not out	9	....
	B 3, l-b 2, w , n-b 1, ...	6	B , l-b , w , n-b , ...

Total 400   Total ....

FALL OF THE WICKETS.

1-2	2-104	3-242	4-268	5-289	6-289	7-336	8-388	9-388
1-	2-	3-	4-	5-	6-	7-	8-	9-

BOWLING ANALYSIS.	First Innings.					Second Innings.					
	O.	M.	R.	W.	Wd. N-b.		O.	M.	R.	W.	Wd. N-b
Ellis	21	...	89	... 1	...	...	...	...	...	...	...
Cranfield	27	... 4	89	... 0	...	....	...	...	...	...	...
Parker	24.1...	5	101	... 3	...	... 1	...	...	...	...	...
Toogood	43	...10	...115	... 6	...	....	...	...	...	...	...

GLOUCESTERSHIRE.	First Innings.		Second Innings.	
1 Mr. M. A. Green	lbw., b Rushby	0	c Hayes, b Hitch	13
2 Smith	b Hitch	4	lbw., Fender	1
3 Cranfield	c Abel, b Hitch	21	c Strudwick,b Fender...	2
4 Langdon	b Hitch	6	b Fender	36
5 Board	lbw., b Fender	23	c Strudwick, b Hitch ...	1
6 Mr. F. H. B. Champain	not out	17	run out	1
7 Mr. C. O. H. Sewell	c Hobbs, b Hitch	10	b Fender	165
8 Parker	b Fender	2	c Hobbs, b Fender	9
9 Ellis	b Fender	0	not out	4
10 Toogood	b Hitch	12	c Hayes, b Fender	2
11 A. N. Other	absent	0	absent	0
	B , l-b 4, w , n-b 1, ...	5	B !8, l-b 8, w , n-b 4, ...	30

Total 100   Total 264

FALL OF THE WICKETS.

1-5	2-5	3-27	4-55	5-63	6-74	7-83	8-83	9-100
1-1	2-9	3-20	4-40	5-198	6-239	7-257	8-257	9-264

BOWLING ANALYSIS.	First Innings.					Second Innings.					
	O.	M.	R.	W.	Wd. N-b		O.	M.	R.	W.	Wd. N-b
Hitch	13.3...	1	44	... 5	...	... 1	12	... 1	63	... 2	 4
Rushby	6	... 0	19	... 1	...	....	7	... 0	36	... 0	... . .
Fender	7	... 1	32	... 3	...	...	17.4...	2	83	... 6	... ..
Hayes	...	...	...	...	...	....	5	... 0	35	... 0	... ...
Abel	...	...	...	...	...	....	3	... 0	12	... 0	... ...
Wilkinson	...	...	...	...	...	....	1	... 0	5	... 0	... ...

Play commences 12 o'clock 1st day—11.30 a.m. 2nd & 3rd days.
Luncheon 2 p.m. 1st day--1.30 p.m. 2nd & 3rd days.   Stumps drawn 6.30 p.m.
Umpires—Barlow & Butt.   RESULT—SURREY won by an innings & 36 runs.

Scorecard of Hayes' last match as a Surrey professional, in 1914.
Gloucestershire fielded only ten men, A.E.Dipper having already joined up.
The catching of T.H.Toogood, No.10 in the visitors' second innings, has since
been credited to Hayward rather than Hayes.

of his talents beyond batting, bowling and fielding. He had scored as a schoolboy, later designed a scorebook, was to become a coach and had acted as occasional emergency wicket-keeper.

It was the end of an era in more ways than one. The 'golden age', the apogee of the amateur, the pre-eminence of characters such as C.B.Fry, Ranji and Lord Hawke would be diminished as European social structures crumbled and the weaknesses of a society based on inherited privilege would be exposed in theatres of war as 'lions led by donkeys' and be gradually eroded and slowly replaced by one where merit was of greater account.

On the cricket field that established order had been challenged, albeit not overtly by men such as Hayes, Hobbs and Hayward. Certainly they remained socially inferior and a further half-century would elapse and another world war be fought before the snobbery of the amateur-professional divide was abolished and the artificiality of Gentlemen and Players discontinued.

Notwithstanding that, however, Hayes was asked to captain the Players against the Gentlemen, led by C.B.Fry, at The Oval in July. The professionals won by 244 runs. Pelham Warner with the unquestioning arrogance of his class and generation commented: 'Hayes, of Surrey, captained the professionals with sound judgment. As a general rule, professionals do not make good captains. Hayes is one of the exceptions.'

Rather more objectively, the *Daily Telegraph* reported:

> A feature of the Gentlemen and Players match at The Oval was the undemonstrative captaincy of Ernest Hayes. His management of the bowling was exceptionally tactful, though subjected to a dangerous temptation. He had many bowlers at his command, yet he was never induced to change for the sake of change. He made it quite clear to those interested in such matters why he took the steps that were so successful.

> . . . I have met Hayes on the cricket field in three continents during a large number of years and he has always struck me . . . as a most admirable judge of the game. One cannot say whether it is with him a matter of instinct or training or both, but in his sense of proportion he has few superiors and not many equals. Indeed in that respect he much resembles Wilfred Rhodes.

Praise indeed.

Following Britain's declaration of war on 4 August, the cricket season stumbled to a close. On the first day of the war, Surrey were at the head of the Championship table with 69 points from 18 matches; on 3 August, over 14,500 people had passed through The Oval's turnstiles and saw Jack Hobbs score a double century in the traditional Bank Holiday match with Nottinghamshire. After some indecision, there was a preference for 'business as usual', and the professionals, including Hayes, continued to turn up to play, though spectator numbers fell. In Surrey's case, three matches were transferred to Lord's after The Oval was requisitioned by the army; one of these was Jack Hobbs' benefit match. A depleted side, captained by Hayward even though it included two amateurs, went up to Edgbaston and lost. Then Gloucestershire came to The Oval, but with only ten men, the only instance in the official Championship where a county has been unable to raise a full side throughout a match. Finally in response to rising public concern about cricket continuing, the Surrey committee, with the club still at the head of the table, cancelled the county's last two fixtures. Later, on 9 November, on a day when the newspapers were expressing concern about the failure of the recruiting effort, the MCC committee formally decided to award the title to Surrey.

The Surrey side which took the Championship in 1914.
Back row (l to r): H.Strudwick (wk), A.Ducat, G.J.W.Platt, W.C.Smith,
H.S.Harrison, A.Sandham.
Middle row: J.W.Hitch, E.G.Hayes, T.W.Hayward, D.J.Knight, T.Rushby.
Front row: J.B.Hobbs, W.J.Abel.
C.T.A.Wilkinson, the appointed captain, is missing.

On the Western Front: 1914 to 1919

Ernest Hayes' war is summarised in his scrapbook in half a dozen lines:

> As soon as the season closed I attested for the Army by joining the Sportsmen Battalion [actually – the Sportsmen's Battalion (23rd Royal Fusiliers)[15]] and before going to France had some good cricket with them in 1915. Thank God I am back safe and sound from the war and can now put photos of the period 1914-1919 in this book.
>
> Joined as a private, I became 1st Lieut., was mentioned in despatches 1916 and received the MBE in 1919.

For laconic, modest understatement, that last sentence takes some beating. He received the Victory Medal, awarded to military and civilian personnel who served in a theatre of war; additionally, however, he was entitled to wear on the ribbon of that medal two bronze oak leaves, denoting in each case a mention in dispatches. He also received the British War Medal for service abroad and was awarded the military version of the MBE.

The bulk of the scrapbook contents for this period relates to hostilities on the sports field, rather than those in the trenches and there are more photographs of battalion and regimental football and cricket teams than there are of soldiers in battledress. While in training at Oxford, he captained an Army officers' team against the Isis Club and later, in 1919, wrote to the *British Expeditionary Force Sports Journal* about cricket in France while looking forward to the resumption of cricket in England.

Nevertheless, his war record was a distinguished one, as evidenced not by Hayes himself, but by the *London Gazette* and correspondence received from one of his former comrades. Unlike France and Germany, Britain had no conscript army until the Military Service Act 1916, and Hayes was one of the million who responded to the call of Lord Kitchener, Secretary for War, for volunteers. The 23rd Sportsmen's Battalion comprised men older than the average soldier who, because of their lifestyle, were generally fitter. It seems to have attracted a 'new type of soldier' and was rather more 'cosmopolitan' and less stratified than many

---

15   His medal card says '22/R Fus' which would appear to be a War Office error. The Royal Fusiliers' Website lists the Sportsmen's Battalion as the 23rd, though his later correspondent refers to it as the 22nd.

Hayes, Bill Hitch and Andrew Sandham at the Sportsman's Battalion training camp at Grey Towers, Hornchurch in Autumn, 1914.

The Sportsman's Battalion cricket side of 1915,
including Hitch on the back row, and Sandham, Hayes and Patsy Hendren on the front row.
Most of the men in the unit were amateur sportsmen.

other Army units.[16] There was an upper age limit of 45 so, aged 37 when war was declared, Hayes qualified with some ease. There were problems with uniform, because as well as being fitter than average, many of them were taller than average and there were insufficient uniforms for men over six feet. Perhaps this was less of a problem for Hayes than some of his colleagues. One of his obituaries recalls him as a slightly-built man and *James Lillywhite's Cricketers' Annual* recorded his height and weight, albeit as a young man, as 5ft 9in and 10st 5lb.

E.G.Hayes is listed as No.347 in the nominal roll of original members who joined either at the Hotel Cecil in the Strand or at Grey Towers, just off the High Street in Hornchurch, Essex, where early training, including the digging of trenches, took place. Ian Peebles' book on Patsy Hendren says that Hayes, Hitch, Sandham, and Denis and Patsy Hendren were among the earliest volunteers at the old Hotel Cecil. First recruitment took place on 25 September 1914 and the War Office took over the battalion on 1 July 1915. They landed at Boulogne in November 1915, but some members were held back. Hayes, having taken a commission on 24 August 1915 arrived as part of a reinforcement team on 20 May 1916 - in good time for the Battle of the Somme which was to result in a million casualties. The regiment was then at Souchez; it moved to Carency in June, was on the Somme in July and took part in the Battle of Delville Wood, about fifteen miles east of Amiens, the first time the regiment went 'over the top' out of the trenches. Casualties were heavy - 60% of those taking part, including 13 of the 18 officers, were wounded or killed - and included the boxer, Jerry Delany. One of the battalion's officers, Major N.A.Lewis later wrote of this action: 'One of the Hun officer prisoners remarked that our advance through the wood was the finest thing they ever saw, but that he objected to being captured by civilians.'

In a letter home dated 26 June, Hayes reports two pieces of luck. A week earlier a shell from a big mortar blew out the front of a dug-out in which he and two other officers, one a captain who was wounded in one arm, were sitting having tea. Rescued after forty-five minutes in darkness, Hayes was fortunate to escape with deafness in one ear. In the other instance a piece of shrapnel passed through two pouches and came to rest against his revolver

---

16   The battalion also acquired a reputation for achieving a high morale and maintaining excellent discipline throughout the war; Hayes no doubt contributed to these conditions.

bullets, striking one of them without exploding it. After eight days in the trenches, he appreciated a spell at the back of the lines.

Later he appeared in the casualty lists, though the wound, shrapnel across the face, was a relatively minor one and after an injection, he continued to serve in the trenches. In September, he was promoted to temporary Second Lieutenant and transferred from the Royal Fusiliers to the General List for duty with a trench mortar battery. By June 1917 he was acting Lieutenant and second-in-command.

Hayes claims to have no recollection of an incident in July 1917 – like many who went through the experience of the First World War, maybe he chose deliberately to forget – but nevertheless, forwarded the letter to *MUFTI*, the battalion magazine:

> You will remember that dark, cold and infernally uncomfortable night of the 12th July 1917 when the good old 22nd were lying in shell holes adjacent to the East Miraumont Rock on the Ancre waiting to go over at the first flush of dawn: how we subsequently advanced in the early morning and how in the end we were all gloriously mixed up with the Royal Berks and the KRRs. I was rather badly wounded, having stopped an explosive bullet in the arm, shrapnel in the back and one through the foot. You came along the shallow bit of trench somewhere towards the front which was crowded with machine gunners etc. Half fainting with pain I hailed you as an officer of our battalion. You gave me a strong pull from your flask, which gave me sufficient strength to crawl many hundred yards to safety.

> I was unconscious for many days, but pulled through in the end. Fortunately the hospital people managed to save the arm, although it will always be paralysed.

> J.R.Skimmin, P.O.Box 488, Queque, Southern Rhodesia

Hayes has added the following note:

> I received the letter printed below in August from one of my old comrades in the 22nd RFs and forwarded it to *MUFTI* , the present magazine of the late battalion for old members. I did not remember him, but he had seen my name in a paper sent to him in Rhodesia, and wrote asking about my welfare and any other old battalion friends.

In February 1918, he returned to the Royal Fusiliers as a Second Lieutenant and was demobilised in March 1919, four months after the end of the war, retaining the rank of Lieutenant. By this time the battalion was based near Cologne, part of an occupying Army.

The Surrey Annual Report for 1919 acknowledged his front-line experience:

> Lieutenant Ernest Hayes, who is captaining Surrey this year, has been awarded the MBE (Military Division). He served in France with the Royal Fusiliers, enlisting as a private, and was on one occasion badly knocked about in a shell explosion, being buried for a considerable time.

Chapter Eight

An Officer and a Gentleman – and a Bridegroom

> Peace hath her victories
> No less renowned than war
> Milton, *To the Lord General Cromwell*

1919

Discharged from the army, Hayes rejoined a nation at peace, but one which would be burdened with the aftermath of war for some years to come, and looked forward to the resumption of first-class cricket, albeit played as two-day matches that season – a short-lived experiment.

Surrey had arranged 25 first-class matches, including twenty in the Championship, plus the Gentlemen *v* Players fixture. It was, or so he thought at the time, Hayes' last season in first-class cricket:

> I was demobilized by the Army in March of this year. This proved to be my last season as a first-class cricketer being injured, two fingers on my right hand had, through past hard knocks, which had severed the tendons, bent well over & I could not catch or field well so retired from the game apart from local cricket.

> I finished my career playing as an amateur & had the honour of captaining Surrey for the first half of the season.

Hayes played in twelve matches for Surrey, captaining the team in four early matches, where he was the only amateur in the side. He was eventually succeeded by C.T.A Wilkinson, who had captained the county to the Championship in 1914 and whose return to cricket had been delayed by his war wounds.

In the trial match at The Oval on 10 and 12 May, between Mr E.G.Hayes XI and Mr F.T.Badcock's XI, Hayes had 15 and 90 – Hobbs had 106 and 118 – and was 'glad to find that I could still bat all right'.

However, against the Australian Imperial Forces XI:

> After playing for half an hour, Australians batting, I fell on my shoulder in trying for a catch & strained a muscle so badly that I could not play for weeks. Returning to the side against Oxford University we won by an innings and 47 runs & I scored 40, but could not bowl or throw my shoulder being painful.

It may well be that a separate incident, unrelated to cricket, contributed to the injury. It is known that Hayes was proficient at billiards – according to popular myth the sign of a misspent youth, though there seems no evidence of that in his case – and in his time in South Africa, he had acquired some skills in horsemanship, but an attempt to combine the two skills seems not to have been successful. Under the heading 'A Losing Hazard: A Cricketer's Race Round a Billiard Table', a local newspaper reported:

> Mr Ernest Hayes, the well-known Surrey cricketer, is more skilful as a batsman than as a horseman, particularly when his mount is a Shetland pony.

> This was proved when he accepted a challenge by a Mr H.Knight for a race round the billiard table at a Hounslow hotel. The conditions were that Mr Knight should run and that Hayes should be mounted on Mr Knight's pony.

> The inevitable happened soon after the start. Mr Hayes was thrown. If he was not exactly shot into baulk, he was most certainly 'out of play' and the victory went to the challenger.

His last match for Surrey, his five-hundredth for the county, was an away game against Kent at Blackheath on 25 and 26 July, in which batting at No.5, he scored one and seven. He muses, rather sadly, 'The next match v Kent at Blackheath . . . proved to be my last in county cricket. I had been missing catches owing to my fingers[17] & still could not bowl & throw so therefore decided to retire from first-class games.'

---

17 *Wisden* later attributed this contracture to catches taken early in his career off the fast bowling of Richardson and Lockwood. However, he took rather more off Lees, Hitch and Rushby among quicker bowlers and 'Razor' Smith in the slower department, as can be seen in the Appendix.

His skill at placing the ball had not left him, however, and the Rev A.Macnamara, reminiscing in *The Cricketer* in 1950, recalls:

> One day he was scoring at a rapid rate, placing the ball with amusing unexpectedness. The ball simply did not go where he led the fieldsmen to expect it. By-passed and stupefied they glanced at each other in bewilderment. Then, from an old soldier in the crowd, came the words of a recent war-time song: 'Where did that one go to, Herbert? Where did that one go?' Hayes made many friends and had a quiet and pretty sense of humour.

Unsurprisingly, he hardly bowled that season. Surrey finished fourth in the Championship, though Hayes' own contribution of 451 runs at 28.18, was not particularly significant. The last of his 48 first-class centuries (153) came against Hampshire at Southampton. In this match, despite the contracture of his hand, he added 353 runs with Andrew Ducat for the third wicket in 165 minutes, setting a new county record which remained unbeaten until Darren Bicknell and David Ward scored 413 in a four-day match at Canterbury in 1990. In the first session of play on the second day, Hayes added 129 runs to his overnight score and Ducat 167. In the match following, against Sussex at Hove, he became only the third Surrey player, after Hayward and Bobby Abel to score 25,000 runs for the county.

Until the First World War, he had continued to play for Honor Oak whenever his county commitments allowed and would now have more opportunities to do so. His elder brother Chris also played and was second eleven captain for a number of years.

Although he was to play no more for Surrey, he remained on the list of 'available amateurs'. He had been a member of the club since 1915 – he had been an employee until 1914 – and remained one until 1923.

1920 and 1921

Compared with other workers who can perhaps expect to work to the age of 60 or 65, professional sportsmen have very short careers - some of them well paid and glamorous ones - which end when they have still thirty or so years of useful working life ahead of them. A number have been so well paid that they need never work again, but financial considerations aside, there remains a psychological void which needs to be filled.

However, despite the benefit system, more significant in days before today's wider availability of pension schemes, most cricketers have generally entered their post-retirement years, needing to do something else to earn themselves a crust. In the nineteenth century it was even more difficult and many were faced with the prospect of 'the workhouse or the river', a number dying by their own hand.

Nowadays, the ECB, the PCA and the players themselves are alive to these issues and there are more opportunities available in radio and television punditry, administration, and coaching. Umpiring has always been open to former cricketers, but not all are temperamentally suited to it. At the time Hayes retired from cricket, the beginning of inter-war economic depression, the licensed trade and coaching were among the options. He tried both with no small degree of success, having failed with a sports accessories business, Louis, Hayes and Co, at 10 Sandland Street on the corner of Bedford Row, just behind High Holborn in Central London. Nothing remains of it now, the site being occupied by an office of the Open University. Contemporary advertisements include a range of equipment, including balls, spikes and batting gloves. One aspect was successful, however, the 'Ernie Hayes' Scoring Book' which remained on the market for a number of years.

As a consequence of his business failure, with no immediate prospect of regular employment, he approached the Surrey committee who, in November 1921, agreed to liquidate the funds from his benefit invested by the Club's trustees on his behalf in the Union Pacific Railroad Company.

Having always been involved in charity work, particularly in the form of end-of-season charity matches for local hospitals, he became Honorary Secretary of the Blinded Soldiers' and Sailors' Appeal. It was not a post he held for very long, however, relinquishing it on his later appointment at Winchester College and being succeeded by G.L.Jessop, whose approach to batting was not dissimilar from his own.

He was still capable of making a significant contribution to club cricket, however, and for the first time in two decades, played regularly with Honor Oak, although he had appeared for them

Advertisements from the 1920s for Hayes' short-lived sports outfitting business and for his rather more successful cricket scorebook.

intermittently whenever he had the opportunity to do so. One newspaper pressed for a comeback after an outstanding performance when he was guesting for City of London in 1920. Under the headline 'Surrey Could Do With Him' it reports: 'Ernest Hayes, who served Surrey well for many seasons, is playing finely in club cricket. He turned out on Saturday for City of London against Hounslow and in addition to making 122 not out took six wickets for 18 runs.'

A return to county cricket was not an option, of course, the levels of skill and fitness for six-day-a-week cricket being quite different from those enabling a player to get by on Saturday afternoons.

Winchester College: 1922

Hayes, clearly accepting that his first-class career was over, covered a couple of pages of his scrapbook with a summary of his career, listing his first-class centuries, all but three of them for Surrey, and adding a further 30 for Honor Oak and other teams. There was no money in club cricket, however, at least not in the unleagued south with its amateur ethos, and following the failure of his business, he was doubtless relieved to accept in 1922 a position of coach at Winchester College with its two and a half centuries of cricket tradition in succession to Schofield Haigh who had died the previous year. At the college his coaching was under the direction of Rockley Wilson, a couple of years his junior, who was still turning his arm over for Yorkshire in the August holidays. Douglas Jardine, with whom he was to work at Surrey a decade later, had left the school three years earlier. In his time at Winchester, Hayes helped bring on the talents of J.L.Guise, who first played for Middlesex shortly after leaving school in 1922 and G.S.Grimston, who played for Sussex from 1924.

Later in 1922 he returned to Honor Oak, played in the cricket week, had four fifties in four matches, and later 131 against Bromley Town and 181 not out against W.T.Cook's XI in an hour and twenty minutes in a mid-week fixture. He continued to play in end of season charity matches, for example for a Wimbledon and District team against J.B.Hobbs' county team for the Wimbledon and Nelson Hospitals.

The *Athletic News* lapsed into nostalgia:

It appears most unlikely that anything more will be seen in first-class county cricket of R.H.Spooner or E.G.Hayes. The latter's career, most of us had assumed, had already ended so far as great matches were concerned, and the statement that he has accepted the position of coach at Winchester College apparently removes any likelihood there may have been of his reappearance in the Surrey team.

. . . mention of Hayes recalls many a vigorous and plucky innings played against odds. He was – none more so – a great-hearted cricketer, never regarding a game as lost until the winning hit had actually been made, and never losing courage while the last hope of his side remained to be dismissed. As bowler and fieldsman he was also the most variable, and he was in addition, a player who was a great credit to his profession. ... Winchester is to be congratulated on obtaining the services of such a player, and for every good reason, it is to be hoped that the engagement will last for many years.

The journalist was correct in his assumptions about R.H.Spooner, the Lancashire amateur and opening batsman, and frustrated in his hope that the Winchester appointment would last a long time. Other challenges would be taken on board.

Away from the cricket field, Hayes was fortunate to escape with his life at an accident at Wimbledon railway station. A local journalist tells the story under the heading 'Ernest Hayes' Close Shave':

I saw Ernest Hayes, the famous old Surrey and England cricketer, yesterday. Hayes never forgave me for always arguing that he played with a cross bat – and so he did – but his wonderful quickness of eye, foot and wrist counterbalanced that defect. He told me that he had had a very narrow escape in the Wimbledon accident. He had just bought his ticket and walked towards the man who 'punches' them when the train came crashing in and left the buffers. 'Worse than the bombs in France,' said Hayes, who was one of the Surrey men who did really good work . . .

India: 1922/23

Hayes had no plans for the winter, so accepted with some speed when the former Middlesex professional Frank Tarrant asked him to join a touring party to India 'partly as his secretary and partly to play cricket and coach where possible'.

The Indian experience, while enjoyable and educational, was not a financial success, two people on whom Tarrant was relying failing to come up with the goods. Hayes records that the Maharajah of Cooch Behar, on whom Tarrant was depending to engage him as coach, had gone to England to seek treatment for brain trouble and died there. Ranjitsinhji had promised work at a college, but decided to stay in England.

So, no coaching appointment, but an opportunity on the way out and back to win prizes of brooches, cigarettes and cigarette cases at bull board, deck quoits and deck tennis. The journey out was smooth, the journey back less so, storms in the Bay of Biscay delaying the arrival by two days. In between, however, there was the chance to play a bit of cricket and see something of the country. Hayes was particularly impressed by Eden Gardens in Calcutta, a very fine city, he thought, with:

> a magnificent open grass space for recreation called the maidan. There are miles of it and it is divided up amongst the different cricket, tennis and football clubs of the city.

> The Calcutta Cricket Club themselves have the finest ground situated in the Eden Gardens & here the turf is properly looked after and the wickets quick and good. The wickets on the maidan are rough and dusty the turf being of a loose kind.

Tarrant and Hayes, with more time on their hands than they had anticipated, joined the Dalhousie Club. Matches were played on Sundays between 11.30 am and 5.00 pm, with an hour's break for 'tiffin'. It comes as little surprise, therefore, that there were few definite results. Nor is it a matter for astonishment, as in South Africa and perhaps slightly less so in the West Indies, that the Indians had their own clubs, such as Mahomedan Sporting and, rather curiously, Aryans.

Winchester again: 1923

Re-appointed by Rockley Wilson at Winchester for the three months of the summer term, Hayes represented the staff against the College first eleven in 1923, a fact meriting a brief mention in the scrapbook, but a report of reasonable length in the College magazine, *The Wykehamist*. Hayes made 61 in a tight draw as the staff just failed to overhaul the total of the Lords, as the school team styled itself. One novel feature was that in response to the perpetual debate in cricket circles about the balance between bat and ball and in particular correspondence in *The Times* suggesting that the bat was becoming over-dominant, the experiment of a fourth stump was introduced. On a shirt-front of a pitch which caused the reporter to suggest that the groundsman would be a candidate to prepare pitches for timeless Tests, it seems to have made very little difference, never caught on and was soon confined to the vast archive of cricket curiosities.

The public schools, of course, reflected in many ways the curious class distinctions of English society, but Hayes, having played through the amateur-professional divide during his twenty-season first-class career seems to have surmounted that barrier with ease. Interestingly, there is an item totally unrelated to cricket in an adjacent column which describes one way in which the class-barrier was broken down. Two hundred public-school boys had attended a military training camp with a similar number of factory workers:

> Each must have wondered a little what 'the other people' would be like; each modestly resolved perhaps to be generous to the faults which so clearly existed on the other side, but after a few days of life together, with class distinctions obliterated by the levelling influence of shirts and shorts, and a common enthusiasm for games, 'the other people' soon became a meaningless phrase. Those who came prepared to break down a barrier popularly supposed to exist, found that it melted away without being touched at all.

Whatever lessons might have been learned from the exercise, they do not appear to have crossed the page where both school and staff, including future cricket historian H.S.Altham, have full initials, usually two or more, occasionally four, with the odd 'Rev' and 'Hon' thrown in and Hayes, appears simply as 'Hayes'. All the members of the staff team were, of course, simply employees of the school.

Later that year, his school commitments over, he continued to score runs for Honor Oak in the handful of matches in which he played, including 114 against Forest Hill. Against Heathfield, he made 89 from a total of 219 and took three wickets for seven. It was in this year that schoolboy Henry Cotton, later to achieve world-wide fame in another sport, was scorer for the club.

On 28 June, aged 46, at the Hammersmith Register Office, Hayes had married. His bride was Lily Mignon, divorcée of Edward Mignon, who had played 140 first-class matches for Middlesex and a few for MCC before the war. She came with a ready-made family, Edward, known as Ted, aged 12, and George who was five at the time. Ted did not emulate either his father or his step-father on the first-class scene, but went on to play club cricket, not at Honor Oak where he would doubtless have suffered from comparison with Ernest, but at neighbouring Addiscombe where he was a member until well after the Second World War.

Hayes and his new wife and step-sons were able to enjoy a honeymoon in Bournemouth which he commemorated with family photographs in his scrapbooks.

A new life.
Mr and Mrs Ernest Hayes, with her boys Ted and George,
on their honeymoon at Bournemouth in July, 1923.

Chapter Nine
Leicestershire

The years teach much which the days never know
R.W.Emerson, *Experience*

1924

Five years after playing the last of his first-class cricket for Surrey, Hayes returned to the county scene by applying successfully for the position of coach to Leicestershire County Cricket Club. The club had decided, in the winter of 1923/24, to appoint a coach with special responsibility for the first eleven, and bring on new players through membership of the Minor Counties competition. The local newspaper ran a profile welcoming him and summarising the principal achievements of his career. He was back in his natural element and enthusiastic about the appointment and his new responsibilities:

> Although I had enjoyed being at Winchester as coach it was very nice for me again to be among first class cricketers & I enjoyed meeting old friends, who came with the County teams to play Leicestershire.

> I made good progress in bringing on the young players of the Leicestershire staff and hope to make great players of Barry, Shipman and Coulson.

> The cricket grounds of the county are very bad & it is difficult to find likely players. Did not get a lot of batting myself in matches as I captained the Club and Ground team and went in last. When I did I was in quite good form – got 60* v Leicestershire Depôt & 100 for Oakham XI versus Notts Amateurs.

Although formal coaching qualifications were some way in the future, there can be no doubt that Hayes was well-equipped to do the job. Towards the end of the war, he had given *The*

Tollingtonian the benefit of his experience with *Some Hints on Cricket* dealing with the three major aspects of the game. The three attributes of batsmanship are, he says, sight, suppleness of wrists and footwork. He adds: ' . . . every ball bowled must be played on its merits and not by anticipation. Before endeavouring to become a rapid scorer it behoves the batsman to feel that he is capable of keeping his wicket up with both forward and backward defence.'

His critics might say that we have here a case of 'Do as I say, not as I do' and that his failure at times to follow his own advice might have cost him an international career. He goes on to warn against stonewalling: 'which causes so many games to be drawn and creates the feeling that it would perhaps be more entertaining if they exchanged the cricket field for the cemetery.'

Of bowling, he says: 'Having acquired the 'habit' of a good length, try to invent your own way of making the ball 'do things'. Do not be satisfied with the first success; try other means and when you have exhausted every possible means you can think of, sum up the result and then stick tight to the method that seems most likely to bring the greatest success.' And emphasising the importance of fielding, he comments: 'Bad fielding has lost more matches than good batting has ever won.'

The county's playing response to the efforts of their new coach was two extra Championship wins - seven instead of five and a rise of three places in the final table, from fourteenth to eleventh. Leslie Berry and Alec Skelding were brought in as regulars to the side. In the Minor Counties competition the side finished in mid-table.

1925

He had never lost his enthusiasm for playing the game and the following year, 1925, he joined Leicester Town Cricket Club, who played their home games on the County Ground at Aylestone Road. He averaged 33.25 for the Saturday team and 53.37 for the Thursday team and took part in the Skegness festival, as he had in 1924. His charges in the Leicestershire first eleven won seven Championship matches - the same as in 1924 - and finished twelfth in the competition. Haydon Smith was brought into the side as a regular player. Perhaps the coach drew encouragement from the performance of the younger professionals in the Minor

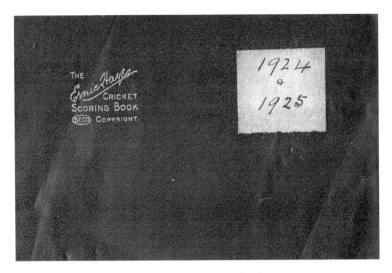

*Cover of a Hayes scorebook
used by Durham County Cricket Club in 1924 and 1925.*

Counties competition, who won five out of eight matches and finished fifth in their table.

He was at the forefront of a debate with MCC on pitch covering. Derbyshire had been censured for engaging in this heinous crime, so other counties had let the matter drop . . . but not Leicestershire. He notes: 'The MCC replied by refusing to give permission for the idea to be carried out. They said that doubtless there were very good reasons from a monetary point of view, but that was not what cricket was played for. It could deprive cricket of the element of chance and thus make it less of a sporting game.'

Surrey would have nothing to do with the idea, but then again Surrey were in robust financial health, whereas Leicestershire, following the dismally wet season of 1924, had a deficit of around £2,000, so attitudes were bound to be coloured. Among his press cuttings are: 'E.G.Hayes, the County coach and former Test player, and Geary, when interviewed both stated that they thought the idea excellent, and one that would be of great assistance to the weaker counties.' . . . 'Geary stated that he thought the game would become more popular as a result of this, and Ernie Hayes said the amount of time saved would be extremely great.'

Later that year Hayes was among the guests at the Savoy Hotel, along with 'a fine collection of great cricketers of past and present days' at a dinner to mark Jack Hobbs' passing W.G.Grace's record of 126 first-class centuries.

In the autumn of 1925, he approached Surrey claiming 'temporary financial difficulty' and asking for help. The committee agreed to let him have 'a sum not exceeding £75 in such amounts and at such times as [the Secretary] may decide after interviewing Hayes'. Because of their own financial difficulties, Leicestershire were clearly not an option. The outcome of the interview and the Secretary's decision is not recorded, but it seems unlikely that Hayes was financially destitute. He was after all in employment with Leicestershire. The likelihood seems to be that he was looking for help in gaining an entrée into the licensed trade, which was eventually to be his main source of post-retirement income.

1926

This year Leicestershire entertained a Danish touring team and, having by this time acquired a residential qualification for the county, Hayes played five matches in the Minor Counties Championship with the second eleven, taking 6 for 42 against Cambridgeshire and contributing 145 towards a victory over Norfolk by an innings and 134 runs. He had last played in the competition twenty-five years before.

With an eye to the future Hayes took a tenancy of the Freeman's Hotel on Aylestone Road and with the help of his wife, Lily, began a profitable business, accommodating most of the visiting counties there.

Then, in early July, a couple of weeks after his 145 off Norfolk, against the odds, in his fiftieth year he returned to first-class cricket. No doubt he drew comfort from the example of J.H.King, who had played regularly for Leicestershire in the previous season at the age of 54. An injury-hit Leicestershire squad was not helped by George Geary's selection for the Gentlemen v Players match at The Oval. The consequence was nothing if not dramatic, if not quite the 'tragedy' reported by the press.

Nottinghamshire won a fascinating game of cricket, successfully chasing over 400 to win the match, but much of the press publicity was saved for Hayes:

. . . a cricket tragedy. Astill, after scoring seven, hit a ball to cover point and started for a run. Hayes responded and was beaten by a quick return from Flint and the wicket-keeper was able to run him out.

Everyone had sorrow in his heart for Hayes who missed a wonderful hundred by a single run. Hayes was batting only an hour and forty minutes to score 99 out of 159. His hits included no fewer than sixteen 4s. No better game has been played for Leicester this season. His display sparkled with all the strokes. He had a great ovation on his return to the pavilion. Hayes set the rest of the side a splendid example.

On the opposing side was a youthful Harold Larwood. He bowled in four-over spells, being 'nursed' for the Headingley Test. The 'bodyline' tour was still six years away, but there is a tidy and satisfying equilibrium in Hayes beginning his thirty-year first-class career against one of Australia's fastest, Ernie Jones, and ending against one who would shortly put Australia to the sword. The press could make nothing of that, but they revelled in the moment:

One Short of a Hundred

Outstanding events of the day, of course, were the brilliant innings of 99 by Ernest Hayes and the dazzling 158 not out by Astill – his highest score in first-class cricket. Everyone will congratulate Hayes for a remarkable achievement, none the less remarkable because his score happened to be one short of a hundred.

A Tall Order

When Hayes was persuaded once more to appear in county cricket at a time when the Leicestershire batting needed a little stiffening, he took on what he knew was a tall order. A 'come back' at anything is an ordeal, and a man of 49, who has been out of first-class cricket for some years, and who has in his time been numbered among the best batsmen in the country, steps into the limelight of a somewhat critical world when he seeks to re-assert his powers in the hazardous field of cricket.

Well, Ernest Hayes on Trent Bridge on Thursday played an innings of which any first-class batsman in his prime might have been proud.

Teaching the Moderns

His style was the forcing style that flourished more in pre-war days than it does today. All the strokes were there. Most admirable of all were the cutting and off-driving that recalled the dashing Hayes of 20 years ago while his vigorous onslaught against the slow bowling of Richmond was an object lesson for the moderns.

Taking the Blame

... run out 99 is always a tragedy. I am glad to have it in the full authority of Hayes that he blames no one but himself.

Astill, just in and perfectly fresh, went for a single for a short one to cover, and if Hayes had been quickly off the mark he would have got in all right. When the damage was done, Astill would no doubt have kicked himself very severely for contributing to such an unhappy incident.

Leicestershire players on the balcony at Aylestone Road in 1926, waiting for the rain to stop. Left to right: G.L.Berry, A.W.Shipman, C.A.R.Coleman, E.G.Hayes, A.Brown, A.T.Sharp, A.C.Lord, G.Geary.

A number of congratulatory telegrams were received and pasted in the scrapbook. Injuries meant that he played another four matches and 70 against Sussex and 45 against Yorkshire contributed to his topping the county batting averages with 254 runs at 36.28; he also took three wickets. It was doubtless with some relief, however, that he was able to record: 'The 'crocks' of the Leicestershire team being fit I retired from the first-class arena this season & I may say that this <u>absolutely</u> finishes my <u>first class</u> cricket career.'

1927

His first-class career now definitely over, he continued as coach to Leicestershire and played in a couple of Minor Counties matches, though with only limited success. He records that he is satisfied that his previous efforts are showing good results and the younger players showing some form. Norman Armstrong and H.C.Snary were now regulars in the side. An article in the *Daily Dispatch* analysing the state of English cricket warned against the dangers of complacency in the wake of regaining the Ashes the previous summer, identifying three faults – an almost total absence of fast bowling, although the Larwood-Voce era was not very far away; an exaggerated attention given to what was then called 'swerve' at the expense of spin and accuracy; and a reluctance on the part of batsmen to hit over-pitched bowling. The half-volley was treated with as much respect as the length ball. To objections that it was impossible to hit modern 'swerve' bowling, the example of Ernest Hayes was cited:

> Last season an old player named Ernest Hayes, aged 50, came out after six years of retirement to bat for Leicestershire against Nottinghamshire. He promptly proceeded to hit up 99 – and even then they had to run him out to get him out – and he did not make his runs by step-in-front-of-the-wicket and deflect-the-ball-to-leg methods. He played exactly as he played before the swerve became a fetish and the googly a bogie. In brief, he hit in the good old way. To my mind the innings was the most significant of the season.

> 'It does show up the young 'uns,' some one said to me at the end of it. It should have done more than that. It should have put the young 'uns' on the right path again.

It was perhaps a tribute to Hayes' coaching that George Geary and Ewart Astill were selected for the MCC tour of South Africa that winter.

An interesting episode was the presentation to Astill by Mr E.G.Hayes, the County Club coach, of a horseshoe decorated in club colours. The horseshoe was presented to Mr Hayes when he visited South Africa with "Plum" Warner's team. It thus acted as a token of good luck a second time. As the two players entered the first-class compartment of the London train Astill held the lucky charm up aloft.

Leicestershire finished the season in seventh place in the Championship, their highest position since 1905. *Wisden* recognised Hayes' contribution to Leicestershire's improvement:

The influence of good coaching on many of the professionals accounted for a large extent for Leicestershire's greatly increased run-getting powers. Nearly all the professionals scored more heavily and had higher averages than in 1926 while Shipman, Armstrong and Bradshaw far surpassed their previous doings. Certainly Ernest Hayes could feel satisfied with the progress of his pupils. Shipman became thoroughly sound in defence, and developing good strokes, scored readily all round the wicket.

He played two Minor Counties matches, both against Staffordshire, whose sides included his old friend and colleague, Sydney Barnes. At Wolverhampton, Barnes took fourteen wickets; Hayes top-scored with 45 in Leicestershire's second innings, the only batsman to show any resistance to the great bowler.

1928

He continued as coach to Leicestershire, who finished ninth in the Championship. At the age of 51 he played three Minor Counties matches for the county and some club cricket with Leicester Nomads, the highlight being an innings of 187 not out at Lutterworth in just over two and a half hours out of a total of 245 for 4.

1929

Leicestershire won nine of their twenty-eight Championship matches and finished the season in ninth place, one above Surrey, despite the greater financial and playing resources of his previous club. At the end of the season Hayes was released, not because of his performance but because of financial exigency. His fate was shared by all the staff except the first eleven and one reserve wicket-keeper. However, he was not job-hunting for long – no time at all in fact. He records: 'Fortunately as soon as this was known, Surrey my old County who wanted a professional coach wired me to go up to Committee meeting and at once engaged me for 1930.'

A smoking concert to mark Hayes' departure was organised, not by the County Club, but by Leicester Nomads some of whose members were also Leicester City footballers. Hayes was presented with a case of pipes and cigarette cabinet and Mrs Hayes with a fountain pen. The Lord Mayor presented him with a Westminster chiming clock. In his valedictory address, Hayes said:

> I put my heart and soul in my work for Leicestershire. Nobody could have taken a greater interest in the club than I have. The committee have never asked me to fill a vacancy in the first eleven without me producing a trained player who has been a credit to them.

> I am very sorry indeed that finance had to step in, but in my opinion the committee probably started at the wrong end of the stick.

> If money must be saved it should not be at the expense of the cricketers, because a club must have capable reserves. There are many promising young players with the club and I would have been very glad if I could have stayed and watched their careers. They will still need advice and counsel and, although experienced men like Geary and Astill still can assist them, there should be someone in the position of head-man to whom they can go.

Mr J.Duncan was more blunt and direct, stating that the county club were making a great mistake in letting Ernie Hayes go. Leicestershire's loss was Surrey's gain. In 1930, the season after he had left, Leicestershire won only four matches and fell to twelfth place in the Championship table. Perhaps the most telling measure of their decline came in the county's last match of the season, at The Oval, where Hayes was now coach: Surrey won by 268 runs, after declaring in both innings.

Chapter Ten
Homecoming

> Fear no more the heat o' the sun,
> Nor the furious winter rages;
> Thou thy worldly task hast done;
> Home art gone and ta'en thy wages.
> Shakespeare, *Cymbeline*

1930

Returning to Surrey after a decade away, Hayes found there had been a marked deterioration. In 1929, Surrey had finished the season at tenth in the Championship, their first time in the lower half of the table since 1904, when they had been without a regular captain. In 1930, they just about crept into the top half by finishing eighth, but secured only three wins under Percy Fender's leadership: their position was due, as much as anything, to Fender's talent for finessing first-innings points out of drawn games.

> I found Surrey very poorly off for bowlers and altho' travelling round the county all the season & having numbers of Young Players through my hands nobody promising turned up. We enjoyed a left-handed batsman named Fishlock who might turn out a forcing player and another youngster named Whitfield promises well.
>
> There is a dearth of bowlers among all clubs, in fact young cricketers are scarce and I think tennis and motor-cycling have a lot to do with it.

Though it is scarcely reflected in his scrapbooks, once he was back at Kennington, no doubt Hayes rediscovered that expectations were far greater than at Leicester. Surrey were one of the 'Big Six' counties, with a catchment population of well over two million people. A far bigger club membership expected their teams to win matches and Championships; to produce Test players whose names were household words from a sizeable professional playing and ground staff; and to stage big matches, some of them internationals, featuring their own players.

He was paid £275 per annum, less than the Clerk, considerably less than the Club Secretary, but probably more than most of the players and acceptable enough at a time of inter-war depression when three million of his fellow citizens were in the dole queues.

His prediction seems to have been right in the case of Laurie Fishlock who in his time also became a stalwart of the county, less so in the case of Whitfield who nevertheless played over a hundred first-class matches. Another of his protégés, Jack Parker, would within a couple of years be commanding a first-eleven place. It is one of those nice little coincidences of continuity that life occasionally produces that the issue of the *South London Press* which reported Hayes' death in 1953 also carried the news of Fishlock's own appointment as cricket coach and physical training instructor at St Dunstan's School in Catford.

Hayes played with Honor Oak on Sundays and had half-a-dozen scores over fifty, as well as 53 for Sandham's XI *v* a Twickenham XV. His last surviving recorded appearance for Honor Oak was against Catford on 9 August 1930, when he was aged 53. According to the *Lewisham Journal*, he bowled, batted and fielded well, then met with a slice of bad luck:

> The veterans, E.G.Hayes, of England and Surrey fame, and Cecil Gibson bowled exceedingly well, the former with wretched luck and both better than their following figures indicate: Hayes 18-1-58-2, Gibson 21-3-88-5. . . . Hayes' catch to dismiss Meikle off a slashing shot was well worth seeing.

> Honor Oak collapsed in an extraordinary manner. The first, second and third wicket all fell at 24, but the fourth, which fell at 49, was the turning point of the game. Hayes never looked like getting out, having scored 24 (five 4s) of the 25 put on when he hit a ball to Greenbaum at mid-off. There was no question of a run, but the latter, seeing the batsman outside the crease, suddenly shied at the stumps. Hayes, to avoid being hit, jumped over the ball and Tyler, gathering the ball very wide of the wicket had the bails off in a trice. It was good opportunism on the part of Greenbaum, a very fine piece of work on the part of Tyler, but extremely bad luck for Hayes.

Surrey re-engaged him as coach for 1931. But, no doubt with memories of his dismissal by Leicestershire, and perhaps as insurance against a time when he would no longer be coaching, he took over the Crown Hotel at Shepperton, to the west of London, as a prelude to his last port of call, the Paxton Arms in West Norwood. As we have seen, he had already had success in the hospitality business in Leicester.

1931

Surrey, led by Percy Fender, in his final season in the job – he was rather clumsily eased out of the captaincy after the season had ended – finished eighth in the Championship. The only new regular player brought into the side was Edward Sheffield, a fast-medium bowler, who was unable to keep a regular place in the side in subsequent years.

It was the last season for Honor Oak on their Colyton Road ground, now acquired for building purposes. To help defray some of the costs of the move to the new ground on Dulwich Common, Hayes took a County XI along to play – and presumably appeared himself – in what, on 19 September, was probably the last game on the ground after 66 years there. No scoresheet has survived, but it

Hayes coaching the younger generation at The Oval in the thirties.

looks as though the county side may not have been a particularly strong one as they were dismissed for 35.

1932

Surrey introduced three new regular players into their Championship side: Freddie Brown, now 'down' from Cambridge University, and Jack Parker and Edward Whitfield from the professional staff. Winning nine matches under Douglas Jardine's captaincy, the side finished fifth in the Championship, though not within striking distance of the four sides above them.

Hayes himself was able to report that the Surrey batting was much improved, Parker's success as a bowler continued and he had some difficulty identifying a captain for the Young Players team.

1933

Surrey finished ninth in the Championship, exactly in mid-table: they won six matches, but *Wisden* characterised the side as 'unreliable'. The scrapbook does not mention it, nor does any Surrey history, but in his last two seasons, Hayes must have worked with Douglas Jardine who captained the county in the seasons either side of the 'Bodyline' series. Although an amateur, Jardine's approach to the game, at least at international level, was nothing if not professional – too much so, some might say – and one wonders at the symbiosis between the professional and personable Hayes and the autocratic amateur whose captaincy in Australia had won the warm approval of the Surrey committee in the form of a congratulatory minute, if not of cricket's establishment as a whole.

Possibly Jardine's view of coaching coincided with that of Brian Clough – it was for kids, not required at the top level of sport and consisted in telling players when to get their hair cut. However, his success with England was not reflected in his county captaincy, Surrey finishing fifth and ninth in the Championship, in the years when he was in charge. Then again, Surrey did not have a Larwood or a Voce . . .

There is photographic evidence of Hayes playing in 1933, though the scrapbook annotation does not say for whom.

1934

Jardine relinquished the captaincy and was replaced by Errol Holmes. Three new regular players came into the side, Laurie Fishlock and E.A.Watts from the professional staff; with Monty Garland-Wells as a new amateur, who joined Freddie Brown and Holmes to form the 'Biff-Bang Boys', intent on playing 'brighter' cricket. Surrey fell to eleventh position in the Championship table, although they won six matches, as in 1933. Jack Hobbs, Hayes' old playing colleague, played a handful of matches for Surrey, bringing his illustrious career to a gentle close.[18]

Hayes records, 'This proved to be my last year's County coaching & my connection with 1st class cricket but I hope still to get some match play with my old club Honor Oak so I am still 58 not out.' He had developed something of a flamboyant life-style – at least in one respect. One newspaper reports that 'Mrs Hayes often fetches him in a sports car painted the Surrey chocolate and bearing the name of the county on the bonnet.'

Perhaps inevitably with increasing age, he felt that 'Fings ain't wot they used t' be'. In an interview with B.J.Evans, he says:

> It is a hard task discovering youthful talent because the boys of today don't take the game seriously enough. They are brought to the ground in cars and their first thought is whether they will be taken home the same way. . . . There isn't enough enthusiasm for cricket among modern youths, and some of the best of them turn to tennis because it is not such hard work.

He was replaced for the 1935 season as coach by Alan Peach. Neither the Surrey minutes nor the annual report contain any appreciation or expression of thanks, so it must be assumed that his departure was with a whimper rather than a bang. However, his *Times* obituary as well as referring to him as 'one of the finest batsmen of his day' goes on to say that 'he helped in the development of many players who later earned Test honours'. Even allowing for a *De mortuis nil nisi bonum* ethos, the compliment seems to be appropriate and well-deserved.

There is no reason to believe that Hayes was dismissed by Surrey, but it cannot be said that he had brought about any great

---

18   At the start of his career, in 1905, the rhymester Albert Craig had described Hobbs as 'Another Ernie Hayes'.

improvement to Surrey's ranking among the counties. The county had made no challenge at all to the dominance of the Northern counties in the Championship, as perhaps supporters may have hoped. Over his five seasons as coach, eight or nine new regular players were introduced into the Surrey first eleven; as at Leicestershire, these were mainly batsmen, perhaps reflecting Hayes' principal skill as a player, but bowlers, essential to match-winning, had remained in short supply. Surrey's second eleven finished the season in the leading group in the Minor Counties competition in all five of seasons when Hayes was coach. They were in second place in three of these. These sides included many of the younger players on the professional staff: for reasons which are no longer apparent, few of these players were converted into players of substance in the first team.

Honor Oak and the Paxton Arms: 1933 to 1953

In 1933, almost as though he was finalising preparation for a 'life after cricket', Hayes took over as the licensee at the Paxton Arms hotel in West Norwood, which he ran with his wife Lily until his death twenty years later. The Paxton Arms was then an ordinary, south London pub, but is now a gastro-pub, re-built and re-named 'The Mansion' and shunted upmarket.

Hayes was licensee of this West Norwood pub, then called the Paxton Arms, for twenty years till 1953.

In 1939, according to *The Cricketer*, while he was making a slow recovery from an attack of duodenal ulcers, he was doubtless cheered by an outstanding century by stepson Ted for Addiscombe – 160 in two and a half hours, with eight sixes and 15 fours.

At the end of the 1948 season, aged almost 72, he was elected President of the Honor Oak Cricket Club, due recognition for sixty years service to the club he had joined as a schoolboy scorer. He served until his death in 1953, but was apparently not often seen there, his duties at the Paxton Arms on Gipsy Road doubtless keeping him away. He was succeeded in the office by his life-long friend, F.G.Cutbush, who had been secretary before the First World War.

He remained in touch with the Surrey club and was present at a dinner at the Armourers' Hall on 29 November 1950, to celebrate sharing the County Championship with Lancashire and winning the Minor Counties competition.

Greetings and a complaint in Sydney Barnes' copperplate, 1953

He died – according to his death certificate – of cardiac syncope, arterio-sclerosis, senile changes and bronchial pneumonia – on 2 December 1953, at the West Dulwich Nursing Home, 30 Alleyn Park, just round the corner from the Paxton Arms. Despite his excursions on overseas tours and to the East Midlands, South London had remained his home stamping ground, within easy reach of his beloved Oval and the Honor Oak Cricket Club. The informant was his step-son, Ted. His widow Lily in the emotionless prose of letters of administration, 'the lawful widow and relict' inherited just over £3,000 from 'the said intestate'. The nursing home no longer exists, demolished and replaced by Kingswood School which in turn became Kingswood Foundation School, a Centre for the Performing Arts. He was to have been an honoured guest at the dinner that evening at the Grosvenor Hotel in Central London, to celebrate the second of what eventually became

Formal condolences from Sir Jack Hobbs, Hayes' playing colleague for eleven English seasons and a friend for nearly fifty years.

Surrey's seven consecutive County Championships. Among the guests at that dinner were Sir Jack Hobbs, with whom the later part of his career had overlapped, and H.S.Altham, now rather better known than when they had been together on the staff at Winchester.

Letters of condolence were sent to his widow by among others, Alf Carpenter of Leicestershire County Cricket Club; B.K.Castor, the Surrey secretary; K.T.Mason, the secretary of Honor Oak; Andy Sandham, Jack Hobbs and Herbert Strudwick, his playing colleagues. His cremation took place two days after his death, on Friday, 4 December, at Camberwell Crematorium in Honor Oak. He was survived by his widow and step-son Ted, who continued at the Paxton Arms after his death.

* * * * *

In his career with Surrey, Hayes as a batsman was almost always in the shadow of better-known colleagues. He contended with the popularity of Abel, the reliability of Hayward and the prodigious talent of Hobbs. To the South London faithful, he was perpetually a *medioxumus*, a deity of intermediate rank. His difficulties as a Test batsman confirm this status. But he fulfilled a special role for Surrey as a batsman: he often had the specific task of forcing the scoring along. Opponents rarely found it difficult to score runs at The Oval in his day, so that rapid run-getting was always a Surrey priority if matches were to be won, and his endeavours often cost him his wicket early in his innings.

As a wrist-spin bowler, he had a handful of seasons in mid-career where he made an important contribution to the Surrey attack; oddly, some of his best years were cold, wet seasons, when conditions were at their most adverse to his methods.

His exceptional talent as a slip fielder has perhaps been forgotten. Only Stewart *père* has taken more catches for Surrey. In the thirteen seasons from 1899 to 1911, Hayes was among the leading five catchers in the Championship in all but three. In his early career, when off-theory was king and when few captains put a fielder behind the wicket on the leg side, he had the job of chasing the ball down to that boundary – and it was a long way down to the Vauxhall End in those days. So he was a runner, too.

His all-round skills – there were few matches where he failed to contribute to the outcome in terms of runs added or dismissals achieved – indicate a man of energetic disposition. Indeed the full story of his life, including his travels when a young man, suggests a character who filled 'the unforgiving minute with sixty seconds' worth of distance run', the Kipling phrase so much a manly precept of his era.

In his time, professional cricketers on retirement typically became publicans, or coaches at public schools, or sports outfitters. Hayes, apparently adaptable and adventurous, undertook all three of these activities after 1920: for about ten years two of them concurrently. He was still 'in harness' at his Norwood pub shortly before his death at the age of 77. The commercial background of his upbringing on the Old Kent Road thus had its legacy.

His distinguished war record and his rise to commissioned officer status suggest that he was a man of considerable leadership qualities. Had injury not supervened and had conventions been different, he might well have been the appointed Surrey captain from 1919; as it was the Surrey club availed itself of his skills only rarely and in emergencies, recognising his merits even before the Great War. The confident tone of his scrapbooks suggests clarity of thought which would have helped him motivate mature players and develop the talents of apprentices. His coaching tenures both at Leicester and Kennington were perhaps short, but there can be little doubt that he brought on the batsmen among his charges.

Albert Craig, the Surrey rhymester and supporter of Hayes' benefit in 1908, regularly told his listeners that all the players were gentlemen and all the gentlemen were players. Hayes was one of many for whom the distinction between amateur and professional was immaterial: indeed his obituaries underscored the point. *Wisden* carefully avoided any prefix to his name: *The Times*, perhaps acknowledging that he was 'officer material', awarded him a proper heading 'Mr E.G.Hayes.' It had been a long journey from Peckham to Norwood.

Acknowledgements

Very special recognition is due to Ernest Hayes' family, who recognised that our subject's scrapbooks would one day have a value to historians, and in particular to his nephew, Christopher Hayes, now deceased, who presented his scrapbooks to Surrey County Cricket Club's library, thus making them available to researchers.

My own thanks are due to Mark Ramprakash, now with 103 first-class centuries under his belt, for contributing his foreword on his Surrey predecessor; to Maurice Alexander, for much detailed information on Honor Oak Cricket Club and Hayes' involvement with it; to Vicki Clark and Polly Rhodes for checking the first draft of the manuscript; to Suzanne Foster, Winchester College archivist, for information on Hayes' time at the College; to Jo Miller, Members Liaison Officer at Surrey County Cricket Club, for her help in the library generally and reproduction of illustrations from Hayes' scrapbooks in particular; to Peter Wynne-Thomas for providing me with information from his unpublished index to *The Cricketer*; to Brian Hunt and Durham County Cricket Club for examples of the Ernie Hayes' scorebook; to Mike Spurrier, for his expertise on military decorations; and to my wife, Jennifer, for her customary assiduous and detailed research and proofreading help.

My thanks are due also to staff at the British Newspaper Library, Colindale; the Southwark Local Studies Centre; the Surrey Cricket Library at The Oval; and the Surrey History Centre, Woking for assistance in their various ways.

In the production of the book, thanks are owed to David Jeater, the editor of the series for refining and amplifying the text; to Philip Bailey for his help with statistical questions; to Peter Griffiths for his typesetting and other aspects of its printing; to Zahra Ridge for her cover design; and to Raymond Hart and Gerald Hudd for their proofreading.

Bibliography

(a) Regular Publications

Cricket: A Weekly Record of the Game magazine
The Cricketer
Cricket Star
Crystal Palace and Norwood Advertiser
Daily Dispatch
Daily Express
Daily Mail
Daily Telegraph
Lewisham Journal
James Lillywhite's Cricketers' Annual
London Gazette
Morning Leader
Norwood News
South London Mail
South London Press
Sporting Life
The Sportsman
The Times
The Wykehamist
Wisden Cricketers' Almanack

(b) Books and Articles

M.B.Alexander, *A History of Honor Oak Cricket & Lawn Tennis Club 1866–1965*, Honor Oak Cricket Club, 1965

M.B.Alexander, E.G.Hayes: A Heart of (Honor) Oak, *Journal of the Cricket Society*, 2, 1964

W.A.Bettesworth, Chats on the Cricket Field: E G Hayes, in *Cricket* magazine, 16 July 1908

Robert Brooke and Philip Bailey [eds], *First-Class Cricket Matches 1896* [and other years to 1914], ACS Publications, various years

Brian Cowley [ed], *Surrey County Cricket Club First Class Records: 1846–2000*, Surrey County Cricket Club, 2001

Bill Frindall, *The Wisden Book of Cricket Records*, [Fourth Edition], Headline, 1998

C.B.Fry, *The Book of Cricket*, Newnes, 1899

Arthur Haygarth, *MCC Cricket Scores and Biographies: Volume XV*, Longmans and Co, 1925

Jack Hobbs, *My Life Story*, The Star Publications Department, 1935

E.R.T.Holmes, *Flannelled Foolishness*, Hollis and Carter, 1957

Dennis Lambert, *The History of Leicestershire County Cricket Club*, Christopher Helm, 1992

Tony Laughton, *Captain of the Crowd*, Boundary Books, 2008

David Lemmon, *The History of Surrey County Cricket Club*, Christopher Helm, 1989

Sir Henry Leveson Gower, *Off and On The Field*, Stanley Paul, 1953

Anthony Meredith, *The Demon and the Lobster*, The Kingswood Press, 1987

Louis Palgrave, *The Story of The Oval*, Cornish Brothers, 1949

Ian Peebles, *'Patsy' Hendren*, Macmillan and Co Ltd, 1969

Ric Sissons, *The Players*, The Kingswood Press, 1988

E.E.Snow, *A History of Leicestershire Cricket*, Edgar Backus, 1949

Richard Streeton, *P.G.H.Fender: A Biography*, Faber and Faber, 1981

F.W.Ward, *The 23rd (Service) Battalion, Royal Fusiliers*, Sidgwick and Jackson, 1920

(c) Websites

www.cricketarchive.com, www.thefusiliers.org, www.umich.edu

Appendix
Career Statistics

Test cricket: Batting and Fielding

		M	I	NO	R	HS	Ave	100	50	Ct
1905/06	South Africa	3	6	1	69	35	13.80	-	-	1
1909	Australia	1	2	0	13	9	6.50	-	-	-
1912	South Africa	1	1	0	4	4	4.00	-	-	1
Career		**5**	**9**	**1**	**86**	**35**	**10.75**	**-**	**-**	**2**

Test cricket: Bowling

		O	M	R	W	BB	Ave	5i
1905/06	South Africa	9	1	28	1	1-28	28.00	-
1909	Australia	6	0	24	0	-	-	-
Career		**15**	**1**	**52**	**1**	**1-28**	**52.00**	**-**

Note: Overs in all Hayes' Test matches were of six balls.

First-Class cricket: Batting and Fielding

		M	I	NO	R	HS	Ave	100	50	Ct
1896	England	5	9	2	152	62	21.71	-	1	6
1897	England	4	7	0	113	50	16.14	-	1	2
1898	England	13	16	2	256	38	18.28	-	-	9
1899	England	28	41	1	1058	131	26.45	1	8	28
1900	England	27	40	1	1248	175	32.00	3	6	28
1901	England	29	51	3	1400	121	29.16	3	7	39
1902	England	35	53	2	1167	114	22.88	1	2	40
1903	England	35	61	7	1865	145	34.53	3	11	41
1904	England	34	58	2	1903	273*	33.98	3	13	43/1
1904/05	West Indies	9	16	1	425	100*	28.33	2	1	8
1905	England	36	62	5	1997	189	35.03	3	12	35
1905/06	South Africa	8	14	1	186	35	14.30	-	-	8
1906	England	35	56	5	2309	218	45.27	7	11	54
1907	England	32	53	1	1857	202	35.71	3	9	35
1907/08	Australia	11	14	0	230	98	16.42	-	1	8/1
1908	England	32	44	0	1119	136	25.43	1	8	45
1909	England	37	65	5	2161	276	36.01	3	11	38
1910	England	22	33	1	1008	88	31.50	-	8	36
1911	England	33	54	6	1827	137*	38.06	4	9	35
1912	England	31	46	1	1812	143*	40.26	4	8	18
1913	England	26	46	1	1377	161	30.60	2	8	29
1914	England	21	34	1	1143	134	34.63	4	5	19

1919	England	12	16	0	451	153	28.18	1	-	8
1926	England	5	7	0	254	99	36.28	-	2	3
Career		**560**	**896**	**48**	**27318**	**276**	**32.21**	**48**	**142**	**607/2**

Notes: Hayes was dismissed 487 times caught (57%), including 81 by known wicket-keepers; 236 times bowled (28 %); 84 times lbw (10%); 21 times stumped (2%); and 20 times run out (2%). He was dismissed more than twelve times by E.G.Dennett and W.Rhodes 16, by G.H.Hirst 15, by T.G.Wass and C.Blythe 14, and by A.E.Trott and J.T.Hearne 13. Four of these eight were left-arm. The bowlers from whom he took most catches were W.S.Lees 102, W.C.Smith 62, J.W.Hitch 50, T.Rushby 47, T.Richardson 37, W.H.Lockwood 30. Hayes played 500 matches for Surrey, scoring 25,062 runs at an average of 33.10, and taking 560 catches. On nine occasions, Hayes held 35 or more catches in a season for Surrey; no other player for the county has achieved this.

First-Class cricket: Bowling

		O	M	R	W	BB	Ave	5i	10m
1896	England	1	1	0	1	1-0	0.00	-	-
1897	England	53	14	121	5	3-3	24.20	-	-
1898	England	154	37	351	15	5-22	23.40	1	-
1899	England	96.1	18	292	9	3-22	32.44	-	-
1900	England	4	0	14	0	-	-	-	-
1901	England	39	10	99	3	2-44	33.00	-	-
1902	England	145.4	22	431	20	4-26	21.55	-	-
1903	England	196	41	534	18	4-82	29.66	-	-
1904	England	419	83	1124	42	6-48	26.76	1	-
1904/05	WI	121.2	25	325	26	3-16	12.50	-	-
1905	England	591.5	110	1771	76	6-51	23.30	2	-
1905/06	SA	32	5	123	2	1-18	61.50	-	-
1906	England	332.3	49	1091	43	5-11	25.37	1	-
1907	England	337	83	932	23	4-75	40.52	-	-
1907/08	Australia	46	1	193	5	2-35	38.60	-	-
1908	England	261.3	55	718	34	4-19	21.11	-	-
1909	England	353.3	66	1072	48	7-34	22.33	2	-
1910	England	88.5	11	235	12	4-24	19.58	-	-
1911	England	264.5	29	1000	25	4-42	40.00	-	-
1912	England	458.5	89	1438	60	8-22	23.96	3	2
1913	England	344.5	60	1145	33	5-57	34.69	1	-
1914	England	179	36	609	12	5-34	50.75	1	-
1919	England	7	0	45	0	-	-	-	-
1926	England	28.2	6	91	3	2-28	30.33	-	-
Career	**5-b**	**304.1**	**70**⎫						
	6-b	**4252**	**781**⎭	**13754**	**515**	**8-22**	**26.70**	**12**	**2**

Notes: Until the end of the 1899 season, overs were of five balls; they were of six balls thereafter. Hayes took his wickets at the rate of one per 52.47 balls and conceded runs at the rate of 3.05 per six-ball over. Of his 515 wickets, 218 (42%) were caught, including 50 of them by known keepers); 193 (37%) were bowled; 73 (14%) lbw; 29 (6%) stumped; and two hit wicket. He took the wickets of four batsmen more than five times; these were J.T.Hearne 7; and C.Charlesworth, G.H.T.Simpson-Hayward and J.A.Cuffe, all 6. For Surrey, Hayes took 473 wickets at an average of 26.97.

First-class cricket: Centuries (48)

Score	For	Opponent	Venue	Season
131	Surrey[2]	Australians	The Oval	1899
150	Surrey[1]	Worcestershire	The Oval	1900
104*	Surrey[1]	Leicestershire	The Oval	1900
175	Surrey[2]	Hampshire	Bournemouth	1900
121	Surrey[1]	Oxford University	The Oval	1901
100	Surrey[1]	Warwickshire	Edgbaston	1901
108	Surrey[1]	Leicestershire	The Oval	1901
114	Surrey[1]	Middlesex	Lord's	1902
102	Surrey[1]	Worcestershire	Worcester	1903
145	Surrey[1]	Lancashire	The Oval	1903
105*	Surrey[2]	Leicestershire	The Oval	1903
273*	Surrey[1]	Derbyshire	Derby	1904
104	Surrey[1]	Yorkshire	The Oval	1904
100	Surrey[1]	Warwickshire	The Oval	1904
100*	Lord Brackley's XI[2]	Barbados	Bridgetown	1904/05
100	Lord Brackley's XI[2]	British Guiana	Georgetown	1904/05
105	Surrey[1]	Essex	Leyton	1905
189	Surrey[1]	Derbyshire	Derby	1905
152*	Surrey[2]	Worcestershire	Worcester	1905
155	Surrey[1]	Leicestershire	The Oval	1906
147	Surrey[1]	Hampshire	Aldershot	1906
218	Surrey[1]	Oxford University	The Oval	1906
126	Surrey[1]	Cambridge University	The Oval	1906
105*	Surrey[2]	Sussex	Hove	1906
153	Surrey[1]	Middlesex	Lord's	1906
122*	Players[2]	Gentlemen	Scarborough	1906
104	Surrey[2]	Nottinghamshire	The Oval	1907
202	Surrey[1]	Middlesex	The Oval	1907
157	Surrey[1]	Leicestershire	The Oval	1907
136	Surrey[1]	Sussex	The Oval	1908
276	Surrey[1]	Hampshire	The Oval	1909
106	Surrey[1]	Essex	The Oval	1909
144*	Surrey[2]	Northamptonshire	Northampton	1909
109	Surrey[1]	Derbyshire	Derby	1911
137*	Surrey[2]	Warwickshire	Edgbaston	1911
123	Surrey[2]	Lancashire	The Oval	1911
101	Surrey[1]	Somerset	Taunton	1911
100	Surrey[1]	Northamptonshire	The Oval	1912
116	Surrey[1]	Nottinghamshire	Trent Bridge	1912
143*	Surrey[1]	Essex	Leyton	1912
117	Surrey[1]	Lancashire	The Oval	1912
161	Surrey[1]	Hampshire	The Oval	1913
144	Surrey[2]	Gloucestershire	Bristol	1913
129	Surrey[2]	Somerset	The Oval	1914
125	Surrey[1]	Yorkshire	Bradford	1914
103	Surrey[1]	Lancashire	Old Trafford	1914
134	Surrey[1]	Yorkshire	Lord's	1914
153	Surrey[1]	Hampshire	Southampton	1919

Notes: Hayes scored centuries for Surrey against all other Championship counties of his time but Kent. He never scored two centuries in a match, the nearest being 97 and 105 v Sussex at Hove in 1906, and 95 and 104 v Nottinghamshire at The Oval in 1907. Hayes' partnership of 371 with Hobbs against Hampshire at The Oval in 1909 remains the record for Surrey's second wicket.*

First-Class cricket: Five wickets or more in an innings (12)

Bowling	For	Opponent	Venue	Season
13-4-22-5	Surrey	Sussex[2]	The Oval	1898
24.5-48-6	Surrey	Derbyshire[2]	The Oval	1904
26.1-3-117-5	Surrey	Hampshire[2]	Aldershot	1905
18.2-3-51-6	Surrey	Cambridge Univ[2]	Fenner's	1905
8.4-2-11-5	Surrey	Gloucestershire[2]	The Oval	1906
29.4-4-94-5	Surrey	Lancashire[1]	The Oval	1909
15.4-1-34-7	Surrey	Middlesex[2]	Lord's	1909
17.5-6-22-8	Surrey	Gloucestershire[1]	The Oval	1912
17-2-79-5	Surrey	Gloucestershire[2]	The Oval	1912
31.3-0-100-7	Surrey	Worcestershire[1]	The Oval	1912
21-3-57-5	Surrey	Northamptonshire[1]	Northampton	1913
14-4-34-5	Surrey	Somerset[2]	The Oval	1914

Notes: *The index figures [1] and [2] in the two tables immediately above indicate the innings in which the feat was achieved.*

First-Class cricket: Ten wickets or more in a match (2)

Bowling	For	Opponent	Venue	Season
13-101 (8-22 and 5-79)	Surrey	Gloucestershire	The Oval	1912
11-132 (7-100 and 4-32)	Surrey	Worcestershire	The Oval	1912

Sources for all seven tables: First-Class Cricket Matches, various years; and www.cricketarchive.com